HOW TO WRITE A BOOK:

TAKING THE PLUNGE INTO NON-FICTION AND CONQUERING YOUR NEW WRITER FEARS AND DOUBTS

HOW TO WRITE A BOOK:

NON-FICTION FOR NEWBIES

LAUREN BINGHAM

CONTENTS

Non-Fiction for Newbies

How to Write a Factual Book and Actually Kind of Enjoy It

DOWNLOAD YOUR FREE 5 WRITING EXERCISES NOW!

If you're interested in learning to write books, chances are high that you've tried before and gotten stuck. As a result, you may be even less enthusiastic about trying again. If that's the case, check out some personally selected writing exercises from author Lauren Bingham's vault of helpful tricks and tips for getting the cursor moving again... or for the first time. Go to https://subscribepage.io/5-Writing-Exercises to download your own copy of Lauren Bingham's Five Favorite Writing Exercises.

How to Write a Book:

A Book for Anyone Who Has Never Written a Book (But Wants To)

Lauren Bingham

CONTENTS

INTRODUCTION

"... And that's how Uncle Lester became known as 'The Amazing Flying Parcheezi!'" You finish your story with a flourish as the crowd that has slowly gathered around you gasps and giggles admiringly, while a smattering of applause slowly fades.

"That was a great story!" someone says.

"Your stories are always so good," another person intones. "You should write a book!"

You blush a little, embarrassed that your off-handed story about your off-the-wall uncle had garnered this much attention. "Well, maybe someday," you mumble, waving off your newfound celebrity. "Maybe someday."

Sometimes that's where the dream ends. You wander back off to work, continue socializing at a cocktail party, or go back to doing whatever it was before you had to spin one of your amazing yarns. But sometimes it's not that easy. You begin to let your mind wander further and further into the hereto-unexplored territory of becoming a published author. It starts with a little nudge like "If I wrote a book, what would it be about?" Then maybe you creep stealthily into "Who would the main characters be?" Before you know it, you've got three plot points scoped out and have made several mental notes to yourself to research whether situation A is possible, whether product B was available in 1957, and to call your mother, because you can't remember Uncle Lester's middle name.

It happens to all of us. Once upon a time, I was encouraged to write a book. And, well, you see how that turned out. I didn't just wake up, type out a manuscript, and go on with my life, however. It's been a very long and weird journey from "You should totally write a book," to "Would you sign my book?"

I believe that one of the most beautiful things about humans is the stories they tell. Storytelling has given us names for the stars in the sky and informs us of our past. The stories told by our ancestors have built our world, given us clarity in times of need, and continue to enthrall us as tales from the deepest reaches of the world circulate in written form.

At the same time, many have scoffed at me or laughed when I mention that I'm a writer. At first, that used to offend me, but now I have a stock answer that I think suits me and the purpose quite well: "Do you ever read?"

Reading is fundamental. While some parties argue that the future will be controlled by robots, and learning to read will be as useless as practicing proper handwriting, the fact remains that reading is still at the core of the process through which those robots will be built. Others argue that television and audiobooks will soon make reading obsolete, but again, you can't have television or audiobooks without someone writing a script. Your automatic self-driving car might recognize the road signs without your input, but someone needs to program the car so that it can do the reading for you. Plus, even the lightest of duties, such as arguing on social media, requires at least a moderate grasp of written language. Reading isn't going anywhere anytime soon, and as long as there is reading, writers will have a place in this world.

Therefore, when people indicate that they find writing to be a worthless pursuit, I have to wonder what they're trying to get out of the experience. If your sole purpose in writing is to enjoy the process of committing the words in your brain and the scenarios of your imagination to paper (and/or the screen of some device in modern times), then your efforts will never be in vain. If, instead, your goal is to write a bestseller, get a movie deal, buy yourself a large house, and become extremely popular for your witty Twitter banter, then the chances are very high that your endeavors will be fruitless. Sure, you may be far more talented than the latest bestselling author, but talent is what gets books written. Politics and marketing are what turn them into bestsellers.

If you want to write a book, then write a book. Write a book because you need to write a book. Write a book because you're sick of telling the same story and you just want to email everyone the file and be done with it. Write a book because you don't want anyone to forget about The Amazing Flying Parcheezi. Passion is what makes the project so enjoyable. And if you make any money out of it, so much the better!

Nearly everyone is compelled at some point in their life to turn a thought into a story, a story into a book, and a book into a series. Whether it's a memoir, capturing an oral tale in written format, or weaving a new universe full of fascinating inhabitants who do interesting things, all of us have stories inside us, just bursting out. Writing is what gives us the ability to capture all of these things and draw them out into the open from the deep parts of our brain in which they dwell. How can any of us possibly be unworthy of jotting down our thoughts?

That being said, it's only fair to warn you that writing isn't always easy, and it isn't always fun. There are times when you've stared at a blank page without progress for so long, that you start to wonder if you're still literate. You'll stay up all night and get up before the sun rises because you have to "work out this part here." Your writing will interfere with your life, and your life will dramatically cramp your writing style. But if you want to write, then go do it!

This is not a book about how to write a bestseller. This is not about my journey to the top of the *New York Times* list, because I haven't gone there-- nor do I think I'll ever make that particular trek. The quality of the book you write is entirely up to you. I make no promises, as the saying goes, but I'll tell no lies.

Instead, this book is going to be about the writing process. This tool is intended for anyone who is stuck on the teeter-totter of "should I/shouldn't I" when it comes to writing a book. Instead of talking about things like grammar and kerning, we'll be exploring the work that needs to be completed before you even name your manuscript file. We'll skip the helpful tips for writing a marketable plot, but we'll look at staying organized and focused while your tale comes to life. Rather than going through the steps of finding an agent and shopping for a publisher, we'll comfort and calm those going through the editing process for the first time. Fiction or nonfiction, prose or poetry, there's a little bit of something for everyone when it comes to keeping brains happy and spirits high when attempting to crank out your very first literary attempt.

Whether or not this book convinces you to write your own, you will put it down with a confident understanding of what it takes, emotionally, physically, and intellectually, to write your very first book. While I believe that everyone has a story to tell and a platform on which to tell it, only you can decide whether you have the internal fortitude to get through the process.

There's no judgment, either. If this book teaches you that you are not in a place to write a book this very second, then it's done its job. But, if you find yourself taking notes, brainstorming in a secret notebook, or daydreaming your way through significant moments that would be in your book, then maybe it's time to dip a toe or two into the world of writing.

Honestly, the worst thing that could possibly happen is that you never write a book, and that's pretty much how things stand today, isn't it? Regardless of whether this book is a step towards your new super-stardom as a bestselling author or a precious reminder of why you stick to blogging when you need to exercise your writing chops, you're taking a very big step by getting off of that teeter-totter and finding out what it would take to get the job done.

WHY WRITE A BOOK?

Answering a question with another question is known as "maieutic." In this day and age, it's considered rude, though in Socratic philosophy, it's a necessity. After all, how can we reveal a question's true nature until we have questioned the very question itself? But when you ask yourself why you should write a book, the answer truly is another question: "Why not?"

For many, the process is strange and scary. Even for those of us who have done it a few times, the process remains strange and scary. What if you run out of words? What if you run out of things to talk about? How much time does it take? Am I going to become a recluse? All of those are valid questions, even the "recluse" question. Writing a book can be a very lengthy and passionate undertaking.

There are three main qualities required of those who endeavor to write a book:

1. Time

2. Energy

3. A good sense of humor

Many experts on the topic will say that you need to have a solid plot with intrigue, relatable characters, and a unique writing style to create worthwhile fiction, while nonfiction writers are only deemed good at their art if they write academically and stick to solid facts.

My counter-argument is that while those are very good points, even the most inspirational characters will fail to change lives with their story, and the most accurate factual book in the world will never inform a soul if the author lacks the time and energy to get through the writing process, and the good humor to deal with editing. The worst book in the world is the one no one has written, in my opinion.

So how much time does a book take to write? There's really no set answer to that question. One aspiring author may tackle a topic in segments, researching as they go, and taking their time to flesh out each skeletal section deliberately. On the other hand, some writers have been sitting on a delicious perspective for so long that they can easily type it out in a matter of days, pausing only for meals, bathroom breaks, and double-checking their facts.

Of course, you may have gotten yourself into a situation in which you need to write a book in time to meet a specific deadline. This can be both a blessing and a curse, as you will be forced to trudge along to submit the required assignment, but stressed about keeping yourself on track and able to focus on the topic at hand. There is a certain amount of finesse that is required to set and meet deadlines, and we'll take a look at what it takes to remain cool, calm, and collected in the face of the clock in another section.

If you are writing a book because you want to write a book, and not because anyone is expecting you to do so, then you can plan on it taking as long as it takes. But perhaps, at least for your first effort, you should give yourself a few milestones to complete to keep the process marching along. That could mean deciding where you want to begin and end your book, creating a hypothesis that must be proven, or simply choosing a page number and the date you hope to have that many pages written.

Most writers can bang out a few thousand words per writing session, but they also do a lot of work before, during, and after the writing process itself. The amount of research that can go into a book is absolutely staggering. You might think that fiction lends itself to a little less factual integrity, but you'll still find it's important to find out if your characters can reasonably be behind the wheel of that specific vehicle, based on their time period and income level, or trying to find the right descriptive words for the architecture of the setting you're trying to portray. After all, there's a distinct difference in feel between "Generations of ivy grew unchecked on the facade of the old bungalow, which seemed to crumble before our very eyes" and "Generations of ivy grew unchecked on the glass walls of the skyscraper, giving it a surprisingly cozy ambiance."

Therefore, when you consider the amount of time you're willing to spend on a book, bear in mind that not every moment is going to result in a productive keystroke. You'll backspace, delete, undo, copy, paste, stare into the abyss wonder what you've done, and go back to the drawing board several times. We'll talk about this process in more detail later, as well. But for now, the answer to the eternal question "How long does it take to write a book?" can either be answered with "a month" or "your entire lifetime."

To manage all of this time, you must have energy, as well. Sitting in a chair, typing for hours at a time, can cause all sorts of pain: neck and back pain from remaining seated for so long, wrist anguish from the unnatural position we assume to type, and infinite headaches from staring at a screen for so long. But none of these physical ailments compare to the mental strain of attempting to write a book.

According to many writers-- and actively reinforced by professors, teachers, and many websites on the matter-- you should be able to log 2,000 words a day to be considered an "effective" or "productive" writer   National Novel Writing Month, or NaNoWriMo as it's affectionately known, also encourages writers to exercise their minds and spirit by coughing up at least 2,000 words each day. Truly, this is an admirable number to aspire to, and setting goals is extremely important, as we'll discuss shortly. But there will be days where, as a human with other things to do in your life besides anguish and toil over a simple tome, you might as well wring blood from a stone and find 2,000 entire words that aren't just assorted syllables-- the literary equivalent of noise.

Some may call this affliction "writer's block." I call it what it really is: Running out of energy. Mental, physical, emotional, spiritual... Any deficit in these categories will lead to the brain and hands stubbornly refusing to produce words on a page. And to add insult to injury, you can't just force your way through it, like a profusely bleeding soldier marching stolidly onward through the blasts of fuselage and relentless terror. There are things you can do to redirect what energy you have and possibly conjure up a little inspiration. Every professional writer has their own arsenal of tricks to fool the brain into believing any time is a good time to write, but this is your first book. This isn't your life's devotion (yet). You aren't getting paid (yet). You're just a regular person, writing a single book (so you think) which you'll never do again (so you say). You don't need to know all the professional tips and tricks if you're not going to be a professional, but they can offer you some assistance when you inevitably run out of energy. Should you decide you do need those tips and tricks, you'll find them in the "Helpful Information" section at the end of this book.

As for the last prescription, "a good sense of humor," it should seem pretty logical that the act of writing a book is intensely illogical. Whether you're using a typewriter, a laptop, a quill, or a ballpoint pen, there's nothing simple or straightforward about writing a book. It is simply a necessary activity to which many of us are drawn.

If you don't meet that 2,000-word quota, you need to have the good cheer to simply move on and recognize that Scarlett O'Hara (via Margaret Mitchell) had it right, and "tomorrow is another day." One day might be a 6,000-word day. The next day might yield a mere 6 words. If you overwhelm yourself with the seriousness of being "behind schedule," you'll find yourself creating stress. Stress is best known for its ability to sap all of your available energy. No energy, as we've established, means no book. Don't allow yourself to become stressed.

That's not to say it's important to remain cheerful and delightful every step of the way. The archetype of the artist or creator states that we must be moody and choleric and woeful and always in the throes of romantically piteous agony. My personal suggestion is that you behave as you would normally behave. Just allow yourself a mote of forgiveness if things aren't coming out the way you like.

In fact, for your first effort, I recommend not holding yourself to any sort of expectations. Set milestones, but don't actually carve them in stone. Instead of 2,000 words a day, consider "I'll have gotten through Uncle Lester's childhood years by the end of the month." This way, you have a goal in mind to keep you marching, but it isn't measured by letters or words or hours spent scratching away at your masterpiece. Instead, you can keep track of your progress by your involvement in developing the tale you intend to tell. Making milestones manageable is just one way to keep a sense of humor while you're writing your first opus.

I also strongly recommend that you hold back any urge to edit as you write. Of course, you can backspace or scratch out any misspellings, and if you look at the phrase you've just written and immediately think of a better way to write it, then, by all means, do so. But if you spend every day agonizing over the past 2,000 words, you'll never find the next 2,000 words. Some writers call these "sprints," in which they create a finish line for the day, and simply write, write, write until they reach the finish line. Don't look back; just keep putting one word after another. There will be plenty of time to edit once you've got a full book. In fact, a sentence that looks like utter garbage today might become absolute poetry once you've filled in the paragraphs following it. Provide yourself with enough grace to not micromanage yourself until you've completed the task at hand.

And lastly, on the "sense of humor" topic, I want to urge you to remember that once you have birthed your opus into the world, it will no longer belong to you. It's your original material, of course, and all of the thoughts contained are your own, any likeness or resemblance is purely coincidental and all that, but it is no longer just your baby. Your baby is going to be read by anyone who gets their hands on it, and it's not going to mean to them what it means to you.

That is to say, once the thoughts are out of your head and on paper (or screen, depending on the format), those who consume those thoughts are going to interpret them in their own way. Someone with different thoughts, opinions, experiences, and understandings is going to look at your work and critique based on what they know.

With any luck, your published book will attract the right kind of reader. This is where intelligent marketing comes in, which we'll certainly touch on later in this book. But inevitably, your book will wander into the hands of someone who just doesn't get it. This person will read what they can, and immediately take to the internet to let everyone know that they found your book to be a wad of mindless drivel that is best used to prop up wonky furniture. Not everyone will love you or appreciate your efforts. It's not personal: it's just an internet review.

One of my first books earned a review that said something to the effect of "everything in this book can be found on the internet." It was a "how-to" book. My first reaction was shock and horror. I thought I'd completely failed. Then I really thought about it. The person who wrote that comment wasn't wrong-- everything in the book really could be found on the internet. But when you think about it, that's exactly how the internet works. If you're doing it right, you should be able to verify every factoid in a "how-to" book via the Internet. I'd be more concerned if you couldn't double-check the author's work in a nonfiction scenario, because if the author made it all up, then it's fiction, right?

Regardless of semantics and critics, allow yourself to brush off the harsh comments. Allow yourself to have patience and kindness with yourself throughout the process, from the pre-work to the reviews and beyond. Acknowledge that this is not going to be easy, but accept reassurance from those who have been there before that it is fully rewarding. Be prepared to ride a Tilt-A-Whirl of emotions, and learn when to provide yourself with a little grace.

One of my first books earned a review that said something to the effect of "everything in this book can be found on the internet." It was a "how-to" book. My first reaction was shock and horror. I thought I'd completely failed. Then I really thought about it. The person who wrote that comment wasn't wrong-- everything in the book really could be found on the internet. But when you think about it, that's exactly how the internet works. If you're doing it right, you should be able to verify every factoid in a "how-to" book via the Internet. I'd be more concerned if you couldn't double-check the author's work in a nonfiction scenario, because if the author made it all up, then it's fiction, right?

Regardless of semantics and critics, allow yourself to brush off the harsh comments. Allow yourself to have patience and kindness with yourself throughout the process, from the pre-work to the reviews and beyond. Acknowledge that this is not going to be easy, but accept reassurance from those who have been there before that it is fully rewarding. Be prepared to ride a Tilt-A-Whirl of emotions, and learn when to provide yourself with a little grace.

If you don't, I assure you that you will learn all of these things throughout the process of creating your first book. But it's a lot easier if you get yourself into a good headspace before you even commit the first word to the file.

BEFORE YOU START WRITING

Before you start writing a book, you should know what type of book you want to write. In many cases, that's much easier said than done. Some books lend themselves fantastically to a particular genre or format; for example, "How to Write a Book," is obviously going to be a nonfiction book. I could make the whole thing up, but it's much easier to tell the truth than to reinvent the entire process. Besides, who on Earth would make up a mess like this? But for many authors, you have to decide what to do with your concept before you can go much further.

I encourage aspiring writers to do as much daydreaming at this stage as possible. Obviously, you'll want to tone it down when you're doing treacherous things that require the utmost concentration, such as driving a forklift through a crowded warehouse or guiding a Conestoga wagon over rocky mountain passes. But there are plenty of times when we can put down the phone, tablet, Smart Watch, or whatever you use to occupy your mind when it's not in use and do a little constructive daydreaming. This is how you figure out what your book is really about.

If you're the type who likes chaos, then you'll keep all of this pre-work in your head. If you like to proceed with life in a nice and orderly sort of way, then you might want to have a journal or jot-pad for this. I personally find notes stressful. If I can't live up to my notes, then I feel like I've failed. Therefore, the only written evidence you'll find of my pre-work is my research and my proposed Table of Contents (TOC). In fact, my proposed TOCs rarely look like my final product, so I'm not even sure they can be forensically linked to each other.

When we think about writing a book, we tend to get all tense and serious about it. Instead, approach thinking about a book the same way you think about what you're getting for lunch when you're driving into the office at 7:30 a.m. Dream about it. Make wish lists.

Explore different avenues. Think about the words you want to use. Throw around some concepts you'd like to introduce and how they work together. Words are like Tinker Toys, Legos, Lincoln Logs, or whatever building toy you like to use in analogies-- they fit together in many different ways, so play with them to figure out how you want to use them. Keep your efforts loose and natural so they don't sound forced, stressed, or anxious when you finally write them all down.

It may take you a few days or daydreams to figure out the simple question of "what is my book going to be," as odd as that may seem. In fact, you might consider this your first challenge as an author: to free yourself from your own expectations and write a book that genuinely reflects the message you want to relay to the public.

If you want to write the story of The Amazing Flying Parcheezi, Uncle Lester, then what's the best way to do it? Should you go for a facts-only family memoir style with interviews from the legend himself? Should you write it in the format of third-person short stories, with a little artistic license taken to give the tales a vivid, life-like quality? You could go dark and mysterious, employing the second-person perspective to engage and immerse the reader in the experience. You can include local colloquialisms to drive home the cozy, family setting. You can paint a full picture with lavish descriptions, or you can allow the reader to play with your characters in their own setting by leaving all of the details to the imagination with minimal wordplay. There are so many choices, and they all belong to you.

In the next chapters, we'll look at how to get organized before writing. The first chapter is for those who are ready to walk on the wild side of fiction, while the second chapter is for those who want to stick with the weird things we already know about in a nonfiction format. Allow me to ruin your misconceptions by informing you that neither is easier than the other, and all writers are deeply challenged by the books they choose to write. Regardless, here are some solid points of advice to help you get organized before you get started writing.

FOR ASPIRING FICTION WRITERS

I have nothing but admiration for fiction writers. I have written my fair share of fiction, and I've enjoyed the process, but I always feel a bit self-conscious when I'm done. I end up questioning myself and dragging myself through a rabbit hole of "what ifs." "What if Character A had made a different decision in Chapter 4?" "Does Character B's dialogue make them sound like a giant jerk during the big scene in Chapter 10?" "Do we even need Character C?" "Why did I concentrate so much on describing this thing when I hardly even mentioned that other thing?" Fiction is not for the faint of heart or those who have difficulty making decisions. At least, not without a sympathetic editor.

Fiction writing is storytelling without limits. Your story can take place anywhere, at any time, with a cast of any characters you can imagine. Want to drop off one of today's billionaire playboys in feudal Europe of the 1500s? Do it. Need your characters to head out to space for an important plot point? Have them build a rocket out of car parts. As long as you write it, your readers will follow along.

This is where the notion of genres comes in. According to Merriam-Webster.com, a genre is *a category of artistic, musical, or literary composition characterized by a particular style, form, or content.* Science fiction, romance, fantasy, myth, mystery, horror, and historical fiction are just a handful of examples of different genres. Some stories blend a few different aspects of standard genres; Neil Gaiman's *American Gods* is a highly regarded example of genre-bending.

The fascinating thing about all genres, though, is that each one takes the world as we know it and completely reinvents it. Take, for example, the Harry Potter series. While the story takes place in modern-day England, as we know it, the entire Wizarding society, complete with cultural mores, language, and biological traits has been invented by author

J.K. Rowling. There's enough reality for us to understand the character traits, emotions, and actions of her characters, but the fantasy world is completely from the author's own mind.

Does that mean you have to invent an entire world just to write a good fiction book? Not necessarily, but you have to conjure up enough of a world so that your tale has a place where it can reasonably occur. Even though your fictional world may not be tangible, as an author, you know exactly where Main Street and First Avenue intersect. You know what everyone drives, and where they eat dinner. They get their groceries from one of three supermarkets, though there is a farmer's market in the summer. The snooty people are from one neighborhood, and the "across the tracks" area is marked by a specific geographical location.

So then, what happens if you aren't using a time or place that you're familiar with? Well, you start researching and learn what you need to know in order to create a place of your own. But we're getting just a little bit ahead of ourselves here. For now, we'll settle the debate of "what is fiction?" with "a tale that comes entirely from your imagination, generally subscribing to one or more literary genres."

What does it take to write a spectacular work of fiction that everyone will want to read? You'll need that world that we just talked about-- and shall continue to talk about in greater specifics. You'll need to introduce characters that readers will care about. Those characters will need to be involved in some great conflict, which builds throughout the tale before reaching a climactic turning point, at which point there is some form of resolution or denouement in which all of the dangling threads of your tale are brought to a conclusion.

Sounds really simple, doesn't it? Except if you were to write a story that was as simple as that description, it would be a sentence. "Bill, a good-looking fellow in his early 30s, awoke one morning and nearly fell down the stairs; however, he caught his balance by grabbing onto the railing and continued out the door to his unsatisfactory retail job." By definition, that is a full story, but it's probably not going to sell millions of copies, and the movie would be incredibly short.

Therefore, a good fiction story needs to have more purpose than that. This is where the work comes in, and where many people abandon the idea of writing a book in the first place. There are an awful lot of little hazy details that need to be figured out before you start writing, otherwise, you end up with a whole lot of stream-of-consciousness drivel... unless that's what you were going for in the first place, with all due respect to William Faulkner.

To begin your work of fiction, you will need a character map and a plot outline. Some seasoned writers recommend starting with the characters, while others recommend starting with the plot. Both, in my opinion, are incredibly important, so I find it difficult to ignore one in favor of the other. However, both will need to be outlined and unless you have the astounding skill of being able to write two different things with each hand, you'll need to handle them one at a time.

The Character Map

The character map can be a literal map, as the name implies, or an Excel spreadsheet, or a very organized list. You can use pictures to help you visualize your characters, or jot down the details of their appearance. The point of a character map is to bring out all of the potential characters in your tale and to establish who they are, how they're connected to each other, and the roles they play within your story. There are plenty of templates of character maps available online, some of which I've linked to at the end of this book; however, you also have the option to free-form list this information in a way that makes sense to you.

That last bit-- "in a way that makes sense to you" -- is really crucial for the prework. Your notes need to be thorough enough so that you can glance at them and know exactly what you meant. This can be somewhat difficult if your characters summon you from a deep sleep, or while you're changing lanes on a major freeway, but be as detailed as it's safe and sane to be when making your notes. There is nothing quite so frustrating as looking at your notes to see something vague like "don't forget Elizabeth's hair," only to realize you have not only forgotten Elizabeth's hair but who Elizabeth is in the first place. Instead, something like "Elizabeth, Penn's sister, is always brushing her hair, which is why Penn is implicated at the crime scene when a long blonde hair is discovered on the body" will better serve you to keep everyone and everything organized.

So, who are your characters? Who do you include on your map? Your protagonist, of course, or the hero of your tale. The term "hero" does not mean they have to behave like Superman or Captain America. Instead, this indicates that it is the actions of this person, along with their reactions, that will help develop the plot of this tale. There can be more than one protagonist, although generally speaking, only one steps into the lead role. For example, there are plenty of wizards and witches who keep things moving along in the *Harry Potter* series, but there's also a reason it's not called the *Harry Potter and Friends* series. Young Harry is written into a role that requires some heavy lifting, emotionally speaking, so he is the main protagonist.

Then you've got the antagonist. Traditionally speaking, we think of the antagonist as "the bad guy" or "the villain." This is a bit of a misnomer because the antagonist isn't obligated to be morally evil; instead, this character opposes the protagonist. They help generate and perpetuate the conflict at the center of the story. Romeo and Juliet's parents, for example, aren't inherently evil. They just happen to be participants in a long-standing strife. It's technically the familial feud-- and their participation therein-- that causes the tragic end to the star-crossed lovers' lives. But they are still considered the antagonists of their tale.

Therefore, when you're dreaming up your characters, think less in terms of "good guy/bad guy," and more in terms of "people perpetuating conflicting opinions." It's your choice from there to emphasize the morality or evil of their roles.

Then there are supporting characters. Supporting characters often get a reputation as being afterthoughts or leftovers, but they're actually the main reason the plot moves along in the first place. You could write a novel in which the protagonist and antagonist only interact with each other. However, from the standpoint of the reader, it's often helpful to have additional characters around to keep the story moving forward. In *The Girl Who Loved Tom Gordon*, by Stephen King, a large portion of the story follows a little girl wandering alone in the woods. Yet we know that she has a family waiting for her. Her hopes of being reunited with her family-- the supporting characters-- are what drive the plot forward while she wanders.

Supporting characters do all sorts of wonderful things. They can demonstrate the social norms. They can be sounding boards for the protagonist and antagonist. They can be the voice of reason or the devil's advocate. They can show the readers the truth that the protagonist and antagonist can't see because they're too wrapped up in their own worlds. They can be friends, family, housemates, love interests, or people who have managed to walk into the same shop at the same time as one of the main characters.

So how many characters is the right number of characters? That depends substantially on what you're using them for. A traditional Greek chorus includes up to 50 performers, but there's no particular requirement. As the author, it is your prerogative to give every citizen in town a voice or to simplify your story by limiting the number of speakers with backstories.

There are a few things to keep in mind when it comes to choosing your roster of characters, and the map you create can help you organize these tenets of character building. First, there's a difference between full-blown characters and people who happen to show up in your story. For example, if you have a scene taking place at a grocery store, the elderly lady who asks for assistance in putting a watermelon in her cart, interrupting your protagonist's train of thought, doesn't necessarily have to be a complete character, unless it makes sense to give her a name, a backstory, a full purpose in the plot, a relationship to the protagonist, and a specific role in the overall quest. She can, but that's up to you and how much time you want to spend detailing all of this information to readers if she's never going to appear again.

Next, consider what a potential character will provide to the overall plot. If, for example, you decide to write in the very popular trope of the love triangle, make sure it has something to do with the story. If Matt is trying to decide whether he loves Rebecca or Renee, and the reader never actually meets Renee, then why do we even care about her? What purpose does she have in the story? Unless you very clearly indicate how Matt's resilient passion for the mysterious and unseen force of Renee is impeding his ability to behave appropriately, clouding his judgment, or causing him to do cruel things to Rebecca, for example, then it's really not important for the reader to know very much about Renee.

Furthermore, you don't need to write an entire dossier on each person who steps into the book. That may seem like a direct conflict with the "make the characters count" advice, but it's actually part of the same tip. Try to think of your characters as friends you are introducing to your reader. You aren't going to share every intimate detail you know about them, such as their favorite color is orange, their favorite drink is a gin tonic, and the last time they got a haircut was in February unless all of those details are important to the future relationship between the character and the reader. At the moment that Maya is hanging from the side of a helicopter with a machete, flying towards a burning building, we don't need to know that she was born in a small town in Oklahoma, loves green beans, and once had a pet duck named Pajamas It would be helpful, however, to know that she spent four years training with a Russian gymnastics team as part of her undercover role with the CIA, but how you choose to reveal that information to the reader is up to you as the author.

Lastly, it's always a good idea to give each character an entrance, a duty, and an exit, especially if they do something significant within the plot. That doesn't mean we have to follow them around every day through the entire story, but even the elderly woman at the grocery store can wheel her cart up to the protagonist, ask for assistance, and then dutifully disappear in the "Cereal and Breakfast Foods" aisle. Having someone appear, do something very important, leave a lasting impression in the readers' minds, and then just vanish like they never existed can be very distracting and confusing to readers. They can walk away, get in their car and drive off, go home, or get Raptured up during the climax of your story, just as long as it makes sense within the context of the story for them to stop appearing.

As you can see, there's a lot to organize when it comes to creating characters, which is what makes the concept of a character map so very handy. You can see who is who, when they enter and leave the story, what they contribute to the plot, and what we need to know about them to understand their role. Some very talented writers can do all of this without making notes. I am not one of them. Therefore, I always recommend those trying out this whole "writing thing" for the first time at least start with a character map. If you turn out to be an ingenue, then you haven't done anything to hinder the process, and if it just so happens that you need a little help with the organization process, then you're already set up for success!

The Plot Outline

Alongside the character map, you'll need to create a plot outline. A plot outline allows you to map out how you're going to get from Point A, meaning the first page of your story, to Point B, when the first part of the rising action occurs, to Point C, and so on until you've reached the natural conclusion of your tale.

Before your head starts whirling at the idea of having bitten off more than you can chew, let's step back a moment to look at what constitutes a plot:

1. Exposition or introduction

2. Rising action

3. Climax or turning point

4. Falling action

5. Resolution or denouement

The exposition or introduction is just that. This section of your story establishes where we are, who the characters are, and in a sense, why we care. One of my favorite examples of a very neat and tidy exposition is the Prologue to William Shakespeare's *Romeo and Juliet*:

Two households, both alike in dignity,
In fair Verona, where we lay our scene,
From ancient grudge breaks to new mutiny,
Where civil blood makes civil hands unclean.
From forth the fatal loins of these two foes
A pair of star-crossed lovers take their life;
Whose misadventured piteous overthrows
Do with their death bury their parents' strife.
The fearful passage of their death marked love,

And the continuance of their parent's rage,

Which, but their children's end, naught could remove,

Is now the two hours traffic of our stage;

The which if you with patient ears attend,

What here shall miss, our toil shall strive to mend.

Everything you need to know before the characters take the stage is laid out here. The location is Verona, Italy. We're about to meet two well-to-do families, and their children are going to fall in love. Sadly, it's not going to end well. Shakespeare even does us the favor of letting us know the whole thing should take about two hours to get through.

Your introduction doesn't have to be in iambic pentameter, of course; prose is fine. You also don't have to feel the need to be as quick about it. Depending on the length of your book and the story you're going to tell, you can spend pages upon pages and entire chapters building towards the point of your story, as long as everything you say is important to the journey.

Deciding what's important to the journey is the whole point of the plot outline in the first place. Sure, you can just open a Word document and wing it, but you're going to need to keep track of where all of your characters are at all times, what subplots are unfolding and why, and most of all, you'll need to figure out why your audience cares about all this. Sure, it's fun to write a whole bunch of intimate and outlandish details, but does your intended reader want to read all of it?

Take, for example, Bram Stoker's description of the setting in Chapter 16 of *Dracula*:

"Never did tombs look so ghastly white. Never did cypress, or yew, or juniper so seem the embodiment of funeral gloom. Never did tree or grass wave or rustle so ominously. Never did bough creak so mysteriously, and never did the far-away howling of dogs send such a woeful presage through the night."

While it's true that Stoker used a lot of words here to establish the fact that "it was really creepy outside," he did so for a reason. He's setting the scene with words and phrases that would be meaningful to his intended audience. There was no television or radio at the time. People of his era had a limited understanding of the world around them, bolstered by occasional travel and getting their hands on books such as *Dracula*. These words would have chilled them to the very bone, while readers today might read these words thinking "Yes, yes, it's creepy- just get on with it!"

Therefore, when creating your introduction to your tale, think of what your readers want or need to know about the world they are preparing to enter and hook them in by writing to them in the same tone that you would tell this story to them if you were speaking out loud.

While you should never write a book for anyone but yourself, you should communicate in words that emphasize the message you are delivering.

Once you've made sufficient introduction, it's time to start weaving in the rising action. One common first-time misconception is that the introduction/exposition and the rising action can't happen at the same time. There is no particular formula that states that pages 1-32 should be exclusively expository and the rising action should begin promptly on page 33. Consider how many different types of literature there are, how many genres and styles make up the literary world, and how the very act of telling a story can change shape even as the story unfolds. *Dracula,* for example, is told through letters and diary entries. The Harry Potter series is told in third person narrative. Both of them deal with interweaving the rising action in different ways.

If you recall from earlier, I mentioned that "reading is fundamental," and this is why. To write a book, you must understand books. I'm not suggesting you copy any one author, completely adopt a tone that's entirely unlike your own, or do anything that might skitter into the world of plagiarism. Instead, I'm asking that you read a lot so you can get a feel for how books work. The more you read, the more options you have for understanding how your own book works.

Take, for example, two of the books mentioned so far: The rising action in *Dracula* takes place slowly, in tiny steps, to thoroughly invest and creep out the reader. The rising action in *Harry Potter and the Sorcerer's Stone* takes place all at once when a door bursts open and Hagrid steps in to disrupt everything. The swirling, whirling mayhem that ensues reflects and emphasizes Harry's confusion at this whole new world unfurling before him.

So, let's look back at your plot outline so far. You've got notes on what needs to be covered in the exposition, and then what you hope to achieve in the rising action, and you're not entirely sure how you're going to do that. Some writers like to flesh things out as they create their plot outline. Others-- myself included-- like to get the whole skeleton out before they start adding limbs.

That brings us to the climax, or turning point. This is the point of no return. All of the conflict in your tale so far has brought us to this moment: the final battle, the face-off, the big decision, the crowning moment. It is very easy to shirk away from a big climactic scene. In fact, throughout my scholastic career, I got marks for "not making enough conflict." Your story doesn't have to have a great big bang, but it does need to make the reader feel and understand the difference between "before" aka- the world revealed in the exposition, and "now," or the way things will be after the climax.

Stephen King does glorious battle scenes that really reflect how we deal with our demons, both internal and external. Harry Potter whips out the wand. Romeo and Juliet end their lives in a tomb. Every story has some major event where the main character realizes they can't continue doing things the way they did before, and they make a very important change. Some just do it with magic and poison.

Once you've decided what the climax is going to be, you might suddenly think about all the things that you can include in the rising action to help you get to that point. Write all of those things down, even if they're in conflict with each other and can't possibly make too much sense if all used at once. Your plot outline is about possibilities and potential; you'll make the tough decisions later.

From the climax, you then have to figure out a way back down. Generally speaking, the laws of gravity apply to literature as well as anything else, and the falling action takes far less time than the rising action. Basically, now that you've gone in and shaken everything up by having your protagonist face strife and struggle, you've had the climax, and now it's time to clean everything up.

Long ago, a writing professor told us something very important and logical, which, in our quest for belonging among the literary elite, we had forgotten: The purpose of the falling action isn't to make everything tidy and digestible for the reader. Instead, it is intended to demonstrate how things are different. You spent the introduction painting a portrait of life in the "before times," you spent countless pages building up the drama and tension to demonstrate how change was going to be difficult, and then you've got the climax, in which your protagonist is forced to make some sort of major change. Now the reader needs to know what's different and why.

This falling action leads to a resolution or denouement. This is where you wrap things up for this particular tale. This does not, however, have to be the so-called "end" of things. If you have a sequel or series in mind, you might want to make sure you keep enough metaphorical doors and windows open to allow for the next tale. Another option is the oft-complained-about ambiguous ending, wherein we don't know if everyone went home and had a wonderful day, or if more conflict arose, or if the world in which your characters live simply blinked out of existence. The purpose of the end of the book isn't necessarily to make things all pat and neat, but to provide a finishing point for the story you are telling. While in theory, you could continue writing forever and ever, that's simply not how books currently work.

Ending your book can be very difficult for a variety of reasons. It can be emotional since you've spent hours, days, and months leading up to this point. You might have a hard time figuring out how to get the ending just right so that you've tied up all the loose ends without rushing or over-explaining things. Stay calm. Don't panic. Write what feels like it makes sense. Take a break. Read what you just wrote. Take another break to think it over. Make notes. Revisit and tinker. I personally recommend saving each version of your ending, if you don't use a program that already stores a version history. Don't throw your scribbles into the fire or trash bin until you're absolutely certain you'll never visit them again.

As we wrap up this section on building a plot, I'll share something that is surprisingly not mentioned often in the writing community: All of these things can change. Your first version of your plot outline and the book that you actually wrote may be significantly different. You might start writing according to plan and realize that your antagonist would never do that thing, or your protagonist wouldn't care about a particular situation. It is completely natural to discover new and exciting things about your characters and your story as you're writing it.

More importantly, you must quell any negative reaction you might have to these changes. Let it happen. Write it through. Explore where things are going. If it ends up being totally out of scope or making you unhappy, go back to where you feel things took a wrong turn, and go in another direction. Don't stifle your creative flow just because you thought things would go a very specific way. You might just find-- as many before you have-- that you have more than one story you'd like to tell!

And finally, fear not if you have a lot of questions about the actual writing process after reading this-- we'll get further into those specifics shortly.

Making It All "Real"

So now that you've got all the prospective characters semi-fleshed-out, and you've created a basic outline for what you plan on writing, you've got just two chores left:

1. Write a book

2. Make it good

Super simple, right? This is the part where you might feel equal parts prepared and terrified. This is normal. In fact, that feeling is going to be pretty normal from here on out. Regardless, this is when things start to feel "real." And as a prospective author, it's your job to really make it "real."

So how does an author make a completely fake, invented, imagined, and fully contrived world feel "real" to the reader? Research, obtaining resources, and even conducting interviews.

You might be actively objecting as you read these words. "I'm inventing an entire world! I don't need to do research!" I'm terribly sorry to burst your bubble, but everyone needs to do research. Everything you imagine is based, in some part, on what we recognize and understand in this reality. The time it takes your characters to travel from one imagined location to the next city is going to be based on your understanding of distances and the speed of travel as we know it, even if they use a mode of transportation specifically invented by you at this exact moment. From the type of dwelling they live in to the color of their planet, to the distance to the nearest star, you're going to need at least a sliver of reality on which to base your imagination. And you know what makes for a good imagination? Thorough research.

That's not to say that everything in your story has to be absolutely accurate. Readers will forgive a cheat here and there if they even notice at all. But when you're describing people, places, situations, animals, and even the food on the table, it helps if you have a clear mental picture of what you're describing. And mental pictures are formed by experiencing a lot of different people, places, situations, animals, and so on. Therefore, taking the time to research these points will help you gain a broader view of the possibilities, which can in turn help you describe them in rich detail. The reward is that the reader will climb on board without question.

The suspension of disbelief is necessary for fiction to work at all. The more detailed your descriptions, the more accurate your tour of your new world, and the more "real" everything feels, even if it's not real at all, the more willing your readers will be to drop any preconceived notions and come along for the ride.

Resources can come in many different packages. If you're trying to truly capture the essence of an experience, whether that's traveling cross-country, climbing a mountain, shooting into space, or whatever you fancy, it's a great idea to hear from those who have actually done those things. Blogs, vlogs, and social media groups for those who have an interest in those activities can really help you gain insight into what people appreciate and detest about those activities. When you write about it like it's real, it becomes real. Therefore, take your time to see what that lifestyle entails.

You may wish to conduct interviews, either via phone, in person, or email/direct message/etc. with those who have expertise regarding the things you're writing about. Right now, that may seem like overkill for a fiction book, but it can be incredibly rewarding to get some different perspectives about a particular activity, lifestyle, scenario, or aspect of your book that you have limited experience or understanding.

In my own experience, I once contacted a gentleman I met through mutual friends regarding his car. I have driven many cars in my life, but I have not driven a 1971 Buick Riviera. This fellow had a 1973 Riviera. We took it for a spin, and I asked him questions about the maintenance, the steering, and the gas mileage, and he even let me push all the buttons. I didn't necessarily use every single detail we discussed, but I felt much more confident about the frequency with which I had my character stop for fuel on his drive, and his radio had the same glitch my new friend's vehicle had. It made for a much more believable scene with confident descriptions, instead of vaguely referencing the automobile and hoping no one would think about it too much.

I could wax on eternally about the benefit of doing substantial research, but to avoid droning on, I'll leave you with this thought: If at any time you find yourself wondering how you could make your book just a little richer, your descriptions a little deeper, and your world just a little more immersive, consider heading to the web or popping open a book to go the extra mile with your research.

At the end of the day, what you actually do before you start writing your novel is up to you. I certainly recommend a character map and a plot outline, and I encourage you to do as much research before you get started as possible, but sometimes that little word, "possible," gets in the way. For some writers, the best way to get started is to just sit down and start typing, fill in the character map along the way, and jot down the plot outline as you start thinking of it, scribbling with one hand while the other attempts to type. I, myself, have once awoken with a story that was burning so brightly, that I had no choice but to pull open the laptop at 2 a.m. and start typing everything I could think of. That being said, once I reached the point where the brainworm stopped and I was on my own, you can bet I had my notebook out, writing out everything I knew about the characters and where they were headed.

In the words of one of my mentors, "I don't care how it gets organized, but get some sense in here!" That is to say, if you need to write a bit before you create your map and outline, then do it. I will say, however, that the earlier you start organizing in the process, the easier it will be to continue to stay organized, especially when it comes to little fiddly things, like small but very important characters, or subtle plot details that carry all of the subtext of your story. Set yourself up for success, not stress.

NON-FICTION, PLEASE; I'M TRYING TO CUT BACK

Non-fiction, as the name implies, is the absence of fiction. These books are based on facts and are used to share information to discuss, educate, and raise questions for debate amongst your audience. Many people think of nonfiction as dry and boring, but it really doesn't have to be. Consider these various genres:

- History

- Biography

- Philosophy

- Religion and spirituality

- Politics

- Scientific research

- Business

- Self-Help

- Travel

- How-To

These are just a few of the subjects included in the realm of nonfiction. Non-fiction books can be informative or educational expository writing, persuasive pieces that prove a point, contain arguments that attempt to change the readers' minds, descriptive pieces that take readers to an entirely different time or place, or a narrative of a true event, place, or person. Some people feel that nonfiction should not include opinions or use a casual tone, but get a few pages into a Bill Bryson book or guitarist Slash's autobiography, and you'll see that's not always the case.

Non-fiction books can use a variety of different tones to express their content. The tone an author uses is directly dependent on several factors:

- The content

- The audience

- The intention

The content is your book's topic and the angle you choose to explore. A biographical piece in reverence to Pope John Paul II and a biographical account exploring Billy the Kid's role in establishing the economy of the Wild West would have entirely different tones, due to the subject matter at hand. Similarly, a book detailing how to fix the mechanical pieces of a Volkswagen Beetle and a book guiding you through daily meditation practices would read differently, too.

The audience is also important when choosing the tone of your nonfiction piece. Most people prefer to read books that come across as a conversation with a like-minded friend. If your audience is mostly teenagers, you'll use an entirely different tone than you would writing the business advice of a Fortune 500 CEO.

Lastly, the overall intention of your book will dictate the right voice to use when writing it. The intention is somewhat of a secondary piece to the topic, angle, and audience. Essentially, this is the effect you want your book to have on people. Do you want them to finish the book with a bit of admiration for Billy the Kid? Do you want them to have enough information to write a basic essay on your book for their science exam? Or do you want them to feel like they have a blueprint for the next chapter of their own lives? What you aim to do with your words significantly impacts how you use them.

So now that you have carved out a bit of headspace for your nonfiction book, it's time to do the prework.

Choose a Topic

Choosing the topic of your nonfiction book is possibly the easiest part of the process. Chances are very good that you've had something on your mind lately. Perhaps you've been casually obsessing over a period in history, or you've always been interested in a specific individual who has walked this planet. We all have that "something" that we know a bit more about than the average person.

On the other hand, you may wish to write about something simply because it is unfamiliar, and you want to share your exploration of this new topic with the world, allowing them an intimate look at your learning and growing processes. This is not unheard of, especially in travel books. The journal format is very popular, as it gives others insight into the process and encourages others to do the same.

Your topic may be very broad at first. You might decide to write about pyramids, for example, but that's a vast subject. Which culture? Which continent? Which type of pyramids? You see where this is headed. You can endeavor to write a book that discusses every pyramid known to date, but you're going to need to consider how you plan to do that. A picture and a short blurb of each one? A region-by-region guide with a map and brief history? The possibilities are overwhelming.

Therefore, I recommend you allow yourself some time to really sit and cogitate on your topic. Perhaps you write down the topic you have in mind, in the shortest form possible. Then you give it some thought. Run to the library or do a Google search of that topic, using the same term you did when you wrote it down. Let yourself go down the proverbial rabbit hole. Figure out what you love about it. Learn new things about your topic. Not only will this help you narrow down the points you want to make regarding your subject, but it will also inspire greater confidence that you're heading in the right direction.

Perhaps, however, you're starting with a topic that's already pretty niche. You are certainly permitted to take the rabbit hole journey as well; you might discover new facts that you wish to highlight in your book that bolster the discussion you have in mind. Regardless, write down your very well-specified topic, and start brainstorming.

From the main topic, you'll want to come up with some of the main points you want to make with your book. If it's a biography, what are the main points of your subject's life that you wish to cover? If it's a self-help book, what are the steps that someone must complete to reach the intended outcome? If you're writing a history of a location, what is the timeframe or period you'd like to highlight? While it would be wonderful if someone would write a book about absolutely everything of all time, that's a bit impractical, especially for your first outing.

Take your time with this. I speak from experience when I say there's nothing as frustrating as starting a nonfiction book and realizing about six pages in that there's really no book there. You may find that you can write a compelling essay, but certainly not an entire book. Or perhaps there simply aren't enough resources to allow you to fully investigate the topic. Experts may have just as many questions about it as you do. Go down as many rabbit holes as you need to. Talk to your friends. Get in arguments about it on social media. Whatever it takes to help you really get your topic into focus with enough material to write a complete book on the matter.

My personal favorite format is the outline. Some people prefer maps, swim lanes, or lists, but I love a good outline. I start by typing out the main topic. Then I let the main ideas come out. Under each main idea, I then include the points I would like to make about that idea. From the points, I add my evidence, opinions, or supporting facts. The process takes me about a week because I keep changing it. Sometimes I'll submit an outline to a publisher with notes describing what I think might change. Sometimes I'm completely wrong. The point is that your first outline is rarely more than a good starting point to help you get your thoughts in order.

One thing your outline will reveal is where you'll need more information. You might find yourself winding into a really great discussion area, but in doing so, discover that this is an area where you might need to return to the rabbit hole. Some authors will say that this means you've found a dead end, and you need to go back to the start of the maze. I say this is a great opportunity to reveal your discovery to the readers with the same awe it's giving you at this moment. The fact that you are learning something about which you are passionate may indicate that other individuals have never considered this particular view or aspect of the same topic. You can avoid the unknown, or write it into your discussion because it is unknown.

Once you've got an outline that you're satisfied with, or at least one that doesn't give you massive anxiety, you'll be able to see more clearly what thoughts you have about your topic. From here, you can decide what angle you'll take to discuss your topic.

Explore Your Angle

Another common misconception regarding works of nonfiction is that they do not contain any opinions or bias. This is not true across the board. A travel journal, for example, has no choice but to be written from the point of view of the person traveling. It's impossible to be unbiased when you're writing about your own experiences from your own perspective.

In other cases, however, it's a good idea to remain as unprejudiced as possible with a catalogue-like approach, but that's entirely dependent upon the angle you wish to take.

The "angle" is how you will go about investigating your topic. For example, in this book, I've chosen to go with a very candid, casual approach to the topic of "how to write a book." I chose this angle because I think there are enough formal books on the topic, and I imagine there are quite a few people who need a friendly voice who knows what they're talking about to push them into doing the deed once and for all.

When it comes to your book, will you approach it as a passionate argument? A desperate plea? A scientific study? A historical collage? A gentle coaxing? One example I like to use when explaining different angles is that of the self-help book. Some of us need to be yelled at to get our lives straight. Others of us need to be subconsciously guided by the subtext that allows us to make our own decisions. What style are you going to use to approach your topic?

The angle will also become evident from the outline you have created. You may have originally thought that you were going to do a completely unbiased history of birth control methods, only to realize somewhere in the creation of the outline that you simply cannot avoid including your own emotions and opinions on the topic. That doesn't mean you've chosen a bum topic; it simply means you will need to adjust your angle.

One way to approach your angle is to ask yourself "What do I want my audience to take away from this book?" In the example mentioned earlier, "a biographical account exploring Billy the Kid's role in establishing the economy of the Wild West," do you want them to have a higher opinion of Billy the Kid or a less favorable impression of early American economic values? You can guide the audience to understand the topic in a certain light. You can't necessarily make them agree with you, or change their own appreciation of the topic, but you do want them to feel they understand your own insight regarding the topic. The angle you choose takes the reader on a very specific voyage, so make sure they know exactly what to pack to take the trip alongside you.

Organize Again

At this point, you've chosen your topic. You've constructed your outline. You've examined your outline to get a feel for your angle. Now it's time to revisit everything you've done so far and get it fully organized to create the map of where you're heading.

From your outline, you should be able to create a working table of contents for your book. Your table of contents may not follow the same flow as your final outline, because your angle may have changed how your discussion occurs. Additionally, you may look at your outline and discover it doesn't actually fit the schematics of basic chapters, after all.

Much as your first outline isn't necessarily your final outline, your first table of contents doesn't have to be your last. I simply suggest that you turn your outline into a rudimentary draft of your table of contents to help you discover the order in which you'll be writing your book. In non-fiction, point tends to lead to point, and facts support arguments, which means you might find yourself backtracking if you were to write things in a specific order. Make sure your discussion or argument is presented in an order that makes sense based on your angle. Take your Uncle Lester, for example. The topic of the story is how he became "The Amazing Parcheezi." Perhaps you take the angle that he was absolutely destined to earn this moniker based on events that happened throughout his life. Presenting your details chronologically starting with his birth and continuing through how he lived up to the nickname following its bestowal would make sense, in this regard.

Of course, there are a great many topics that don't lend themselves to any type of chronology. That's why taking the time to reorganize yourself will help you create a cohesive journey through your topic and lend further merit to your angle. I've included a few techniques to help guide you through some possibilities for your own nonfiction work in the Resources section, but for now, consider the overall "case" you're presenting. What is your thesis, or point you're trying to prove (if any)? That should be stated in your Introduction, or at the very beginning of the book. Then think of the facts that lead towards that particular conclusion. Which is the strongest? Which is going to take the greatest amount of time to discuss? Can you create an equally long chapter for each fact, or are some of them technically sub-facts that could nestle closely with a larger, more pressing piece of information?

Putting together a nonfiction book is somewhat like putting together a jigsaw puzzle; however, while a puzzle has a definite singular correct solution, your book does not. The final format that you settle upon is beneficial to you, as it will make the flow of your writing feel much more familiar and be gentle on your brain as you compile your massive piles of facts. At the same time, the organization of your book should make sense for your reader, as well. Your reader doesn't want to be confused, overwhelmed, underwhelmed, or feel like they're losing their mind. For example, if you're bringing up a particular example several times throughout a book, either consider a different arrangement or acknowledge this for your reader. I recall a particular example from earlier in my career, wherein certain aspects of a specific city were mentioned six times throughout the book. On the second mention, I thought perhaps I needed a nap. On the third use, I thought I might be going a little mad. By the fourth time, this information popped up, I actively started flipping through the book to make sure I wasn't losing my mind. Sometimes this is unavoidable, but make sure you alert the reader. And try not to use the same sentences over again. Readers hate that.

You may be thinking that this is a lot of favors for your reader, and that's somewhat true. But what is the purpose of a book if not for the reader? We've discussed the concept of "audience" a few times so far, so you have considered for whom you're writing the book and what purpose you want it to serve. But now I'm telling you that you have to reorganize your entire outline just so the readers will like it.

If you never intend anyone to read your book, then really, you don't need to follow any of this advice-- just go for it! Stop reading this at once and go make your dreams come true!

For the rest of us, however, who at least want our book to go over well at the family holiday party, creating a flow of details throughout your piece is crucial to gaining the appreciation of the reader. Have you ever started reading a book, only to stop halfway through because it wasn't capturing your attention? That experience is exactly why you need to at least somewhat include the reader in the experience of writing a book.

Ultimately, the act of writing is a bit of a compromise between the author and the reader. You're going to write the book you want to write, with the understanding that the resulting product should be something the reader wants to read. And believe it or not, that's usually easier than you might imagine.

Research, Resources, and Interviews

A work of nonfiction will require substantial research. There are always facts to validate, points to prove, and references to include in your work to support your writing.

Even in the case of a personal work, such as a memoir or travelogue, you'll help substantiate your information with factual details. For example, rather than vaguely mentioning that Uncle Lester was born in a summer month at the turn of the century, you'll gain more credibility by saying he celebrates each 29 July. In the travelogue example, you'll greatly aid your reader and yourself by being able to mention where you are, where you're going, and how you're getting there.

There are unknown details about everything, even if you consider yourself a walking encyclopedia on a particular topic. At the end of this book, you'll find a Resources section. I would love to say that those are links that I exclusively hand-picked for my dear readers so they can grow and blossom as writers, but for the most part, they're the materials I used myself to organize my thoughts and make sure I wasn't telling you a bunch of bologna. I truly want you to grow and blossom, which is why I made it a point to share with you only information that I would use.

Since this is rarely a situation where "any old resource will do," it's a fantastic idea to really take your time in the research stage. I personally recommend looking up even the facts that you feel you know for certain, for the mere fact of corroborating your data with multiple resources. For example, I recently wrote a piece about a subject I know so well that I've been certified in it several times. In theory, I could have simply sat down and written a stream-of-consciousness brain dump of everything I know, and it would have been true. But it wouldn't have been good, and I wouldn't have had the facts on board.

Another great thing research can do is remind you of other things that go hand-in-hand with your main points. Sometimes, as writers, our focus is so strictly placed on a particular piece of information that we block out knowledge that goes hand-in-hand with those facts. It's very much a "forest-and-trees" situation, wherein you're drilling down to a certain point so enthusiastically that you forget to mention all of the supporting details that are really important to the cause. Once upon a time, I was called upon to host a dinner for some prospective clients. They were chefs, so I wanted to serve some simple but flavorful foods to demonstrate that I had been paying attention and doing my research on the topic they were pitching to me that evening. I found some very reputable resources, and I followed the recipes to the absolute letter. Nearly everything turned out beautifully, except for one particular dish. It looked nothing like the photos. Instead of looking like a fluffy beige spread, it was a wet, lumpy brown mess.

When my guests arrived, I had no choice but to serve it. I explained the situation and tried to laugh it off. They asked if I had done this and that while making it. I had not. "This" and "that" were not mentioned anywhere in the recipe I had followed. We took a look at my resource together and discovered that in the author's zest for explaining the history and cultural importance of the dish, they forgot to mention that the reader was supposed to peel a certain ingredient at a very specific time in the process.

The moral of this story is twofold:

1. Do not lose focus of a really important fact

2. Double-check your resources

It is far too easy to stop researching when you find the information you want. If something seems a bit untoward, it usually is. If I had looked for another recipe, I would have very quickly discovered the missing data. Instead, I looked at what I had and said,

"Good enough!" While my prospective clients found the whole thing hilarious and hired me anyway, consider how your book will be received by people who don't know you directly and aren't able to hear your apologies and justifications for the error. Write it right the first time and earn the reader's trust for a lifetime.

On the topic of author accountability, resources can always be a bit of a mixed bag. In addition to spreading vast amounts of information, we're more aware than ever that the internet can also make misinformation viral in mere moments. This is another reason I like to recommend fact-checking nearly everything. From updates within the scientific community that invalidate previous theories to updates in details surrounding your topic, it's never a bad idea to see what the community at large believes to be the "truth." Some inaccuracies may be unavoidable-- imagine writing an article about the Golden State Killer being at large on 23, April 2018, just one day before police announced they had arrested Joseph DeAngelo for the crimes. I had the pleasure of writing a long piece about a particular celebrity's emotional quest for motherhood that was published the very same day she announced her pregnancy. The saving grace for my career and that of the publisher of that particular outlet was that the rest of my article was a well-researched compilation of her own words on the matter. I was accused of knowing the future, but that's entirely not true!

Another type of resource that can be both a blessing and a curse is the interview. If you can get a first-hand account of anything related to your topic, it will lend credibility and integrity to your piece. Except for one small problem: Interviewees aren't always accurate. That's not to say that they're all filthy liars, but that we are all but human. We remember things incorrectly. Details can get blurry over time and multiple retellings. We may start to confuse situations and transpose a few ingredients within our memories. And yes, some people are filthy liars.

Additionally, there's an interesting phenomenon in which experts might not agree. I encourage anyone who is conducting interviews to get as much perspective as possible on the topic you'll be discussing before actually starting the interview. If they can't get five out of five members of the American Dental Association to agree on the efficacy of a toothbrush, there's not the tiniest chance you'll find two identical versions of the same event.

If you choose to incorporate interviews in your research process, it's a great idea to get contact information so you can follow up with your subject. You may feel you've had an incredibly thorough discussion, yet as you write, you realize you didn't really catch the tone of a particular answer, or the subtext of a response isn't completely clear. If you have the opportunity to clarify that quote or notion, you'll avoid misrepresenting the truth.

So how do you conduct an interview? First, research. Understand what you're going to be talking to this expert about. The most comfortable, informational, and overall successful interviews are more like conversations than a question-and-answer session. You don't have to reach a level of expertise on the topic, but at least know enough that you can participate in a discussion and ask clarifying questions that make sense. There's the famous example of the interviewer who was unaware that Paul McCartney had been in a band before Wings. Just a little bit of research can avoid awkward scenarios such as those.

Next, make sure you're interviewing your subject in a manner that is comfortable for both of you. I learned early in my career that I am incredibly awkward on the telephone. I'd rather take a red-eye flight to Buxtehude for an in-person interview than participate in a lengthy telephone interview. However, if I send my subject some questions via email, I'm more than happy to have a follow-up discussion via telephone. It's strange; I know.

The process of talking to an expert can be somewhat terrifying. Think of it as a conversation. Prepare a list of questions to get you started, but also jot down a list of points you would like to cover throughout the interview. Don't ignore the humanity of your subject. Phrases like "you must have been surprised when you discovered..." or "what was going through your mind when..." or "what was it like to experience..." can give you loads of insight into the interviewee's relationship with the subject at hand, and put a very relatable spin on even the most far-out topics. I once had to interview an investigator who had solved a serial murder and arrested the killer. I asked exactly one question. The rest of the time, we talked about his role in the crime itself, his headspace since the trial, and his relationship with fellow investigators. At the end of our hour-long chat, he asked if he could contact me again in the future when he was ready to write his autobiography. A good interview can be an amazing experience for everyone involved.

When you're using interviews in your nonfiction work, remember that nonfiction is supposed to reflect reality. The absence of fiction is truth. There are plenty of situations in which parts of interviews are specifically edited, decontextualized, and misconstrued to fit the author's angle. I certainly understand why some writers would choose to do this. To an extent, we all wiggle the truth a bit to get the desired results, both in life and in writing. However, depending on the platform you're using to distribute this not-entirely-true information, there may be consequences. While defamation-- specifically libel-- is treated differently around the world, at the bare minimum it will be a dark mark on your writing career.

Writers have argued since the dawn of the written word whether fiction or nonfiction is "harder" than the other. Having written both myself, I have my own feelings on this matter, but for now, this is going to be one of those debates that may never end. Every author has a comfort zone, which means certain pieces will be much "easier" to write than others. Whether "easier" translates into faster to write, less stressful, minimum research, or bountiful source material and imagination remains in the eyes of the beholder, but some books are indeed pleasure cruises while others are as enjoyable as the tour of the S.S. Minnow. That's not to say that all books are boat wrecks, but that some boats are a struggle from the first word and may turn out very different than intended.

Therefore, reflect back to that "sense of humor" I mentioned as a requirement for writing a book. While I've equipped you with various strategies and tools to help guide you through the pre-work of both fiction and nonfiction pieces, please don't believe that any of these are a "one and done" scenario. Don't fool yourself into thinking you can slot "Pre-work for my novel" on your calendar as a brief afternoon chore. This will take time and energy, as also mentioned earlier. The sense of humor is the manna that will sustain your spirit while you wrestle with the reality of how onerous the pre-work process can be.

How you conduct your pre-work is entirely up to you. Many authors get the entire text laid out-- at least a preliminary version-- before they start writing. Others may find that they've organized them into a good space to write a particular section right this second, which they can edit back in once they've got a final structure in place. Use the method that works best for you. This isn't strictly a knitting project or a quilting project; instead, writing is "the art of letting the muse soar brightly," as a former mentor of mine put it. For your first piece, you may wish to tinker around with your order of operations and structure as you discover what works best for you and your train of thought.

Each book you write will involve a certain amount of experimentation. While doing the pre-work will help you prepare for writing a book, don't feel that everything you've done is carved in stone. As mentioned earlier, you may change some very important details in your book as it develops on the page whether you're writing a fiction piece or a work of nonfiction. When things change, don't feel that you've failed in your pre-work, or that these outlines and hours of research were all in vain. If anything, learning what you don't want to do with your book makes it that much more satisfying when you discover the direction you prefer to take instead.

Whether you end up following these steps exactly or using them as the basis for your own unique process, keep in mind that the goal here is to provide you with direction for your new project. Many first-time authors become frustrated early in the writing process, simply because they haven't done sufficient work ahead of time. The great news is that you can always stop what you're doing mid-sentence, and leave yourself a bookmark or note to return and revisit your notes. Maybe your character map wasn't quite as accurate as you had envisioned. Maybe your angle is slightly askew. Revisit. Regroup. Relax.

You may feel like the pre-work is never-ending, especially if you find yourself revisiting and regrouping more than once. That's not a bad thing at all. It's simply preparing you for the next step of the process, which is setting sail on this monumental voyage. The next step, of course, is to sit down and write a book.

SURVIVING THE WRITING PROCESS

To write a book, begin in a comfortable seated position. Make sure you have a laptop, computer, device, pen and paper, quill and scroll, or whatever media in which you wish to write handy. Close your eyes. Take a deep breath. Exhale slowly. Open your eyes. Write a book. The end.

If only it were that simple! In truth, there will be days when writing comes as naturally to you as breathing or swallowing. On other days, you'll feel nauseated just knowing that the written word exists. There have been times when I've been irked by the label on a packet of snacks simply because it dared to include words and sentences.

The term "surviving" may seem a little dramatic or hyperbolic, but I find that writing is an activity of survival for the author and the piece equally. If you give up on writing your book, then the story does not live on. Equally, if you become so frustrated with the process that you swear off writing anything more significant than your name on a birthday card, your development of passion and talent has terminated. While writing a book is unlikely to be fatal, the knocks you feel during the process might bring an end to the whole endeavor entirely. If you quit, it shouldn't be because continuing would ruin your life, but because you've tried writing, and it's simply not for you.

As always, you'll need time, energy, and a sense of humor, which will apply to the various skills that will help you retain your passion for this project even as the days drag on and words start to lose their meaning. In the following chapters, we'll look at some of the things that help writers retain the desire to write, even if the words aren't coming. They may seem a bit obvious at first, but when you're facing a blank white page, the urge to panic is very strong, especially during your inaugural attempt.

In this section, we'll explore some of the best ways to not panic, stay focused, and keep our eyes on the prize of completing that very first book.

Staying Organized

While it's true that the concept of organization has been mentioned more than a few times already, it really can't be mentioned enough when outlining the process of writing your first book.

The temptation to just open a journal or online word-processing document and start writing will be strong. I highly recommend you follow this urge from time to time, especially when creativity or passion starts waning. The only downfall to this method is that when writing with our eyes closed, we tend to lose sight of where we were trying to go in the first place. This is a great way to get the words flowing, but you might also produce a whole bunch of drivel.

One technique for helping yourself stay accountable when going on these writing sprints involves a little extra organization. Each time you sit down to write, I encourage you to take a few moments to read what you wrote in your previous session. Take a look at your notes, referencing your character map and plot outline for fiction pieces, or glancing back to the final draft of your table of contents for nonfiction writers.

A book, with its thousands of words and hundreds of pages, is overwhelming. It's a long journey full of twists and turns and points and counterpoints. So, try to think of it as an adventure with a destination that's still far in the distance. Imagine you're going to drive a car from Seattle, Washington to Boca Raton, Florida. That's a trip of approximately 3,200 miles, which is approximately 48 hours of continuous driving. Looking at it like that, it seems incredibly overwhelming to take on a trip like that, and you might immediately start looking for the fastest and least expensive flight.

But instead of looking at it as two days of endless driving, remember your humanity. You'll need to stop every so often to eat, fuel up the car, and use the restroom. It's in your best interest to pause once in a while to get a bit of rest, lest your eyes glaze over and your brain goes on auto-pilot. Therefore, it is far more likely that you'll break up the voyage into small, manageable pieces. You'll drive for a few hours the first day, and see how the car is handling. Stop for fuel when you need it, and pop into the station for a drink or snack. Pause at rest areas to use the facilities, walk around a little bit, and maybe take a little nap.

Once you relax and let yourself absorb the beauty of the journey itself, you'll start enjoying it more. Maybe you'll stop at a restaurant that you've always wanted to try. You might choose to wander through town a bit while you're there, dashing into the shops or a little local flavor. Of course, there might be days when it rains, or you're just not feeling the spirit of adventure when you just want to put the pedal to the metal and get on with it, but that's part of the journey, too.

As someone who has made several cross-continental voyages and written just as many books (including a book that I wrote while driving the entirety of the American East Coast), I'm always struck by how similar both processes are. The only major difference is that you can write a book in a stationary position, without leaving the house.

When you open your journal or device and gaze upon that blank page, don't think about how monumental this task is. Don't think about how long it will take you to reach your goal, or how inconvenient it's going to be to make the trip. Instead, break it down into small pieces, just like you would on your road trip.

On your first day of writing, focus on the introduction. Don't overthink it-- just start driving. Tune out the part of your brain that's screaming "This is madness! This is too big! This is going to take too long! You're out of your element!" Lock your mental GPS on the first point you want to make in your book and go for it.

Your introduction is going to set the tone for your book, and if you've created loads of notes during your pre-work, it will be the most honest and forthright thing you write. You haven't had the time to come up with preconceived notions about what you're writing. You haven't developed your voice entirely; you're just pecking along, trying to explain what you're about to write to a reader who has no idea you're even writing a book. The whole process is a mystery at this point. Good thing you have plenty of notes.

Just as you certainly wouldn't attempt to drive from Seattle to Boca Raton without GPS, an atlas, a compass, or some type of tool to help you find the way, the notes you assembled during your pre-work are going to act as a map to guide you through your book. Use this map to help you find your way point-by-point, just as you would make your way across the United States stop-by-stop. Perhaps today you write through Chapter 1, or the point in the plot where the main character is introduced. The next time you sit down, you'll get through Chapter 2, or take the main character to the point where the main conflict is revealed.

Set some very specific points, and write each day until you've completed that portion of your journey. What will make this strategy work, of course, is your ongoing commitment to the organization. When you use a GPS or map to plan a road trip, you plot out your points. You check the roads and get a feel for the highways and byways you need to take to get to your next checkpoint. You don't look to your final destination; you take your time finding your way. You stay with your map at all times. Sure, you might end up following a detour, or discover a more scenic route, but you have a specific place towards which you are heading.

Your pre-work, research, and any notes you make along the way are your map. They tell you where you should go next. Let them do their job. Don't leave your notes in a drawer, decide you were out of your mind and throw them away, or tell yourself you can fly without a map. Once you get into a good flow, you might not need your notes every moment, but given that each session of writing is nearly always different from the day before, there will come a time when you'll deeply crave those notes again.

One particular trick that has saved me a lot of time and tears is to keep a writing journal. You might be thinking "I'm already writing, and you want me to write some more? You're out of your mind." It does sound like overkill, I'll admit. But the purpose of a writing journal can be very simple-- to make notes of what you do each day when writing.

By "journal," I don't necessarily mean a bound notebook type of thing, though that system does tend to work for many writers, especially those early in their careers. You can use a system of comments and highlight text in a word processing program, or actual sticky notes if you're handwriting your manuscript. Whatever it takes for you to recognize, record, and revisit points in the process where you had to pause to think about things is as fine a method as any, because you're not keeping a writing journal for anyone but yourself.

Writing is not necessarily a chronological thing, even if the piece you are writing is very strictly chronologically structured. You might be knee-deep in Chapter 12, only to realize that life is going to be a lot easier for your characters if you go back and change something slightly in Chapter 3. On the nonfiction front, you might discover that an argument you made in a previous section was weak where it was sitting, and you clearly need to relocate it to a later section, where it actually enhances the discussion. When you make changes like these, make note of them in your writing journal. Examples of these notes might include things like:

"1, February: Changed April's hair color to brown, starting in Chapter 5. Had her dye it so Rebel doesn't recognize her in Chapter 8."

Or in Nonfiction terms:

"25, October: Moved 'Billy the Kid's horse, etc....' from Section 3: Livestock to Section 7: Tradeable Wares. The livestock section now focuses on cattle and farm life. Chickens going under trade as well, though mentioning them in the "Marketable Goods" section of the Livestock section."

The goal of these notes, and the journal as a whole, is that they will help you not only recognize changes you made in your draft but will also help you remember *why* you did that in the first place. Sure, you can set up your word processing software to track all changes, but it can't capture your internal argument as you try to make a decision.

The concept of organization extends beyond the notes and to the mental notes and dialogue you're having with yourself as you write your book. There will come times when you type out an entire page, then freeze and think "Is that even what I wanted to say?" Being organized in both your notes and your thought process will help you sort out what you're doing. Being able to remain in synchrony with yourself through the days, months, and years it may take you to write a book is the only way I can think of to continue your productivity through thick and thin.

Being Productive

The original title of this chapter was "Staying on Deadline." In my mind, I was going to explain to you how to budget time to get your first draft done within a specific timeframe. But, as I've preached to you frequently throughout this text, changes do happen.

Instead of teaching you how to force yourself to write when your brain says "no" but the calendar says "yes," I'd rather encourage you to develop a passion for productivity. Truly talented writers can spirit up an entire text from nothing in a matter of seconds, but that's not the experience you should have for your first book. Rather, your first book should be an effort you undertake because you truly want to. It should be positive and passionate, and whether or not you choose to ever write another book, you should walk away from the process proud of yourself for having done something so monumental.

You should set a timeline for yourself, as I mentioned earlier, simply to keep your brain aware of the fact that this is a real thing, and it does deserve your attention. How strict you are with your deadline depends on how well you know yourself. Some of us need the pressure to thrive, which means being a little aggressive with deadlines to keep ourselves focused and excited about our writing. On the other hand, you might avoid excess anxiety by allowing yourself generous milestones that simply demonstrate you are making forward motion, rather than wallowing in each potential sticky spot.

Regardless of your expectations, the main goal of setting a timeline is to promote writing. When writing our first book, nearly every writer I've spoken to says the same thing: We start obsessing about whether it's good, interrupt ourselves, rewrite the same paragraph eight times, give up because it's too hard, wonder if we're failures at everything we try, spiral into self-doubt, and basically have a very bad time. Instead of making it good on the first pass, just concentrate on making it.

You want to write a good book, but before it can be good, it must be a book. Write it. Just write the blessed thing! Just like you'd step on the gas and speed away from a roach-infested hotel room on a cross-country road trip, sometimes it's best to keep moving forward and not look back when writing.

Make adjustments. Pay attention to detours. Take the scenic route. But don't spend too much time glancing back at where you've been until you really know where you're going. If you're going along at a nice clip in the introductory pages and suddenly remember that April's hair is going to change color, don't stop. Use that writing journal to make note of it, and keep going. There might be a reason why your brain wanted you to write it this way now. Explore that, but make note of it, in case you don't like where that path leads. You wouldn't turn off your GPS when you got lost, and you shouldn't stop where you are, turn off the car, and call it quits, either. You can always come back when you have more time and fuel.

Remember as you write that when you come back later, you'll have a fuller grasp of what (if anything) needs to be changed. You could go back on April's hair throughout the entire book. What if you discover, just as you're wrapping things up, that April really enjoys changing her hair color, and she does it a few times throughout the tale in order to be more of a social chameleon? You've just realized that you need to revisit every mention of April's hair color to make sure it fits the social situation in that scene. Things like this happen, so make notes and come back later; go forward for now.

You'll also need to examine your relationship with the word "progress." Earlier, we discussed how the recommended 2000 words each day might not make sense for you, at least not daily. I encourage you to gauge progress not by how many words you write each day, but by the things you actually accomplish when you do sit down to write. If you only write 100 words, but you manage to get yourself through a section that was particularly troublesome for you, that's progress! If you do a 4000-word sprint because you haven't had the time to sit down and write for yourself in weeks, that's also progress!

Many people get a little frenzied during their first attempt to write something substantial. If discipline helps you thrive, then by all means, create a stringent program for yourself. I find that if my deadlines are too far in the future, I will almost dare myself to wait until the last minute. But, if I choose instead to force myself to make some form of progress each day, I procrastinate less and I love my final product more. That being said, giving myself a very specific quantity of words to accomplish each time I sit down would exacerbate my anxiety. I'm more of the "write until your head is empty" type of writer when I have my druthers.

Writing in a professional capacity has helped me learn how to hold myself more accountable to a schedule, but hopefully, your first book won't come with a tight deadline!

In preparing for your first book, though, you may not really know what your style is like. You may have never sat down and written thousands of words at once, or if you have, it may have been long, long ago. It's not the type of thing everyone gets to enjoy in their personal or professional life, so it may feel very strange at first.

In fact, it might quite literally feel strange, as in physically uncomfortable. If you're not familiar with typing, your fingers and wrists might become sore or achy after a particularly long stretch of typing. Handwriting your book can also lead to aches and pains in the wrists and fingers. If you don't usually sit for hours on end, your spine and posterior may start to object to your new pastime.

Keep in mind that writing is actual exercise, for your mind as well as your body. Just as you wouldn't enter a marathon if you've never jogged down your driveway, you'll need to give yourself time to adjust to this new activity, both mentally and physically. You might find yourself feeling exhausted at the end of a writing session, or wired from a burst of endorphins as you try a new task. No one told me about how writing can affect the body, so I was completely surprised when I burst out crying inconsolably for half an hour after submitting my final draft. Your brain will be taxed. You might forget things. You might find yourself on edge. You might find it difficult to sleep or to rise. These are all very real side effects of writing your first book.

Over time, the process will become easier, but you need to train yourself to endure it. Take breaks to avoid actual writer's cramps. I like to get up and walk around the room every thirty minutes or so. I wait until I've reached a good stopping point, of course, but then I close my eyes, do some desk stretches, and get up for a good minute or two. Sitting on an exercise ball instead of a regular chair is a great way to avoid the pitfalls of poor posture when seated. In the Resources section, I've included a few links to exercises you can do to keep your body as limber as your mind during the writing process.

Sometimes, if I find my mind blank, I'll turn to the internet and read something related to my topic, just to get the brain juices going. When I was writing heavily for the automotive community, I would pause work to watch episodes of *Top Gear* or *Rust Valley Restorers* to refresh my appreciation of writing in the right tone and voice. Don't beat your poor brain into submission over this task; instead, let be a part of the instrument and play for the muses naturally. Alternatively, I'll shut off the computer and do some Yoga Nidra to prevent my brain from going into overdrive. Find what helps you think-- I've included a few suggestions for brain-cleansing activities in the Resources section. It's important to cleanse the mind from time to time to keep your mental focus and emotions in check.

Give yourself time to focus on learning your own process. By emphasizing the overall accomplishment of any progress at all, you're giving yourself the room you need to learn your own needs. Your procedures will start to fall into place as you become more familiar with your mental, emotional, and physical needs. Make adjustments. I can't tell you how many playlists I auditioned before I found the exact tunes I need to be productive.

Seasoned authors across the board recommend finding a good place in which you can do your writing. A quiet spot, where no one can bother you and you don't find yourself tempted by too many distractions can be incredibly helpful in inspiring and maintaining productivity. This doesn't mean you need to build yourself a state-of-the-art office unless you truly want to. Many a bestseller has been written at a kitchen table, behind a blanket "wall" in the living room, on a closet floor, or in the dark once the kids have gone to sleep. Part of finding your groove is finding a good place to work. If you find yourself being very easily distracted, move. Set yourself up for success; trying to "push through" a situation that just isn't working will only bring distaste for the overall experience.

Over time, your progress will become a process, and your process will in turn raise your productivity. The muscles that ached and the tears that were shed will all become rarer, as your body learns to sit and the mind becomes accustomed to this exciting task. You'll feel less forced, frantic, and formal and more focused. You'll look forward to your writing time. Knowing that you'll return to a sort of normalcy or even a state of bliss after that first major road bump of entering unfamiliar territory should help you keep your eyes on the prize, so to speak. Travel one stop at a time, but if you remind yourself that you're moving forward, the journey will be all the more enjoyable and rewarding once you've reached its end.

Dealing with Changes

By now, you might be a little confused about the methods I'm prescribing for you: always go forward, except when you turn around and go back, but always make notes about why you did then, then go forward again. That's a pretty accurate description of the writing process, but since this is your first time, I'll try to simplify it a bit.

Always go forward. Progress is good. Write more words, make more of your book appear before you, continue the momentum, and so forth. The more you write, the greater the chance that you'll work yourself through those moments of confusion and self-doubt. Always end the session with more words than when you started.

However, change is inevitable. We must not fear change. You will wake up one morning and realize that you didn't include a certain detail earlier, and you need to add it. Do just that. Note it in your journal, and then continue forward. Don't spend an excessive amount of time re-reading what you've already done, because you've got an entire revision and editing process for that. When you go back to make essential changes, I strongly encourage you to put blinders on to the rest of what you've written, at least for the moment. Make your change, make sure it exists peacefully with the surrounding text, and then return to the prospect of forward motion.

But the concept of "change" isn't strictly limited to parts already written. As you move ever boldly forward, get ready for things to get weird. Your characters may turn out to be totally different from your first impressions. You may find that something you considered irrefutable truth was proven incorrect recently. In this great journey of writing, there will be roadblocks and detours you never intended to take.

So how do you deal with unexpected change, especially when you're supposed to be the one in control here? This is one of the very few scenarios in which I would encourage you, as a writer, to pause briefly. The other scenarios include natural disasters, fire, and medical emergencies, but this is one of the few instances when you have a free pass to stop yourself before you proceed past the point of no return. If you have discovered a major gap in reality, you have permission to stop and regroup.

By "major gap in reality," I am referencing situations in fictional pieces such as but not limited to:

- Your character's personality has changed so drastically, they cannot realistically perform the plot as drafted

- The survival of a character is dependent on your decisions, and you hadn't initially planned to write a mortal departure

- You're reaching the ending far sooner than you expected

- The original ending you planned is completely unlikely

- The genre skipped track on you, and in order to follow the new version, you need to do more research

For nonfiction writers, you might encounter the following, and then some:

- Your main argument is based on a fact that has been proven false

- In writing a particular section, you discovered you have a very unequal distribution of information compared to the rest of the sections

- You're making the same point and argument repeatedly, but not in an informative manner

- You're bleeding a rock with your resources

- Your interviewees stop responding to you, and now you have absolutely no idea how their story ends

As you can see, these are not mere "situations," but occurrences that would require major edits to everything that you have written and will continue to write. Think of it as a subconscious railroad switch, gently guiding your barreling train to another track without missing a beat. You may have thought you were the engineer of this particular train, but surprise! Something happened along the way, and you're in an entirely different place.

This does not necessarily mean you should jump ship and abandon your work. In each case, you can revise the text to suit the new situation, if you feel it is for the better. That means you'll have to revisit your initial plans as well as the developing text in order to find all of the bits that are impacted by this update. Sometimes, you'll find that you can actually tie it all together simply by moving forward. For example, in a situation where my interviewees ghosted me, I was able to take the information they had given me in our first sessions, flip the hypothesis of the article, adjust my gaze a bit, and create an even more interesting article because of my changes. Don't give up. Don't be shocked. Look at your piece and think, "What can I make that's even better?"

But sometimes, you're completely blindsided by the change. You can't understand why a particular character comes across as cruel and narcissistic, because you've always intended her to be the self-sacrificing character. Your heroine is annoying, and it seems like the characters are less and less interested in the rising action each day. In the nonfiction world, you might discover you're practically shouting your text, trying to impress upon your reader how important this detail is, or you're repeating phrases verbatim unintentionally. You might look at your book in utter fear, wondering how on Earth did this happen? Who wrote this?

First, know that this is very natural. It can be a bit unsettling when you look at something you've produced, and it is very much not like you expected it at all. Sometimes what our mind's eye sees is completely exempt from replication in the real world, especially when we add our own perspective to it. It sounds a little scary or supernatural, but the way you feel in your own world can very easily be reflected in what you write. Have you ever cleaned the house angrily, or washed the dishes when you were really happy? The way we feel has a lot to do with how we act, and when the duty at hand is translating your own imagination into the written word... well, a funny thing happened on the way to the paper.

The more you write, the easier it will be to avoid this phenomenon, because you'll recognize how you write when you're mad, sad, lonely, anxious, or slightly tipsy on white wine. There will be subtle changes in your style, and the developments in your text will start to reflect the way you're reacting in real life. We write what we know, and if you're having a bad day, you'll use your characters as a sounding board, or your arguments might become a little more impassioned.

This is another reason why I recommend you keep moving forward as much as possible. The energy you bring to the pages when you write is important for productivity, and it can become very stagnant as you continue forward. If you're dealing with something in your private life, keep writing, even if your original concepts change. Likewise, there will be chapters that bore you. Push forward through this to see what comes out on the other side. Your energy is what will keep a book churning forward. When you stop this energy from lingering too long on something that's already been done, you lose forward momentum. Your energy changes. The moment is lost. See where things go, and if it turns out that the inadvertent turn at the station wasn't for the best, first decide where you can go along this route.

When it comes to writing your first book, something will inevitably change. It may be the contents of the book, or it may be your own perspective. Don't fear change; follow it. And when it becomes clear that you need to reassess, do so. What you build upon your current structure is only going to be better for it. But for the love of everything, make notes about it so you don't lose your train of thought or the steam to continue.

Perhaps this was not the outline of "the writing process" you wanted. You might have been looking for someone to help you put one word after the other. Maybe you wanted to know what the best adjectives are, or how to really use adverbs to spice up your writing. Those are very important things to know as a writer, after all!

While I don't disagree that writing is art with words, I also don't feel like I should be telling you how to execute your art. There is a lot about writing to me-- and to many others who write for a living-- that is still somewhat spiritual or sacred. I don't know why I love doing it. I don't know why it has always come so easily to me. I can't tell you where my brain goes, where the words come from, or how I know exactly how I want to organize things. When a character is engaged in dialogue, I don't know who is really speaking to whom on a subconscious level. What I do know is that I can't imagine a way to force someone to let their brain flow into the written word. You just have to accept that it is your task and try it.

And that, more than anything, is my main piece of writing advice: Try it. Don't look at what you've written and say, "Oh that's crap, and I'll never get better." The first time isn't meant to be good. The first few pages will be awkward. You'll be able to see the cracks where you might've stumbled and fudged it for a little bit because you weren't quite sure what was happening. Maybe you got hyper-aware and self-conscious and started doing the literary equivalent of stammering. That's OK! That happens all the time! In fact, that's exactly what the editing stage is for.

If you are expecting to produce Nobel-winning content the first time you even try to write, then I formally invite you to get over yourself. Write first, then perfection. Make the book, then make the book better. I'm not saying be lazy-- always give it your best effort and as much energy as you can muster-- but recognize that you are actually expected to go back and make changes.

In the next chapter, we'll learn how "edit" is not a "four-letter word," despite the fact that it does contain four letters. Change is good. Edits are expected. You have an opportunity to clean the entire house before your company comes over, so take advantage of it.

THE EDITING STAGE

According to Merriam-Webster's online dictionary:

Definition of **Edit**

transitive verb

1a: To prepare (something, such as literary material) for publication or public presentation

edit a manuscript

b: to assemble (something, such as a moving picture or tape recording) by cutting and rearranging

edit a film

c: to alter, adapt, or refine especially to bring about conformity to a standard or to suit a particular purpose

carefully edit the speech

Edit a data file

As you read that, you may see that there is nothing in there linking editing to being a worthless writer. Because it's not true. Editing isn't necessary because you're a terrible person who deserves nothing good; editing is an opportunity to make sure what you've written is exactly right.

Somehow, there has grown a perceived notion that editing is bad, and only people who aren't very good at writing make edits. This is, of course, nonsense. If you care enough to swallow your pride, abandon your ego, and re-read everything you've written to make it even better, then you clearly care deeply about your book and want it to be the best it can be.

Also, for those for whom the reality hasn't quite set in yet: Congratulations; you've written a book.

When you reach the editing process, you have officially written a book. Now you get to make it a good book, and you shouldn't view that as punishment for not writing a book perfectly the first time through, but as a privilege for following your passion and making this dream come true in the first place. If you can grind through the long and emotional process of writing the book, then certainly you can go through the thing again with a feather duster and a bit of polish!

Remember: writing a book requires time, energy, and a sense of humor. It is in your best interest to extend these traits through the editing process as well. Let's take a look at some other things to keep in mind when entering and proceeding through the editing phase of your book. And remember: it's just a phase!

How to Ignore Your Instincts and Edit Subjectively

It is all too common to get that sinking-pit stomach feeling when you face the editing phase. You are going to come face to face with your own human fallibility, after all. It's one thing to emotionally prepare for the act of editing, but to actually do the chore is another thing altogether.

There are two typical reactions to facing the emotions that come with the first round of editing of your first book:

1. Tear it apart. Tear it all apart. Burn it down and start over.

2. Put it in a box. Lock it. Throw away the key. Bury the box.

Neither of these are going to help you. Therefore, you need to learn how to ignore your instincts and simply edit your book.

There are different ways of going about it. If you've been keeping a writing journal, one of the first things you can do is read the journal, and then look back at all the parts you've referenced. Make sure April's hair is the correct color at all times. Be certain that Billy the Kid's horse isn't running amok throughout the text. If you changed a plot point or argument in the mid-to-late part of the book, make sure all earlier references have been updated, as well. For those using a word processing program, the "Find" feature can come in very handy here.

Readers can forgive a lot of things and suspend their disbelief significantly, but inconsistencies are just annoying. Avoid annoying your reader. Do a read-through of your book with the specific intention of making sure everything is consistent from chapter to chapter. And by "everything," I truly mean everything. Here are a few examples of things to check for when evaluating the consistency of your text:

- Is your tone and voice the same throughout the book, or did that energy from being in a different mood leak through, as I mentioned it might?

- Does the narrator or point of view of the text remain the same?

- Are all mentions of locations or settings accurate (this is equally important for fiction and nonfiction works)?

- Are all names spelled the same way throughout the text, or are annotations made where names may change purposefully? (Example: Referencing members of royalty is one situation in which individuals may have a given name, a familial nickname, one or more titular names, and so on. Let the readers know all of them, so it's not confusing when you switch between them.)

- Are all personal details, such as outward appearance, clothing/style, personality, and other identifying characteristics unchanging, OR do these details change appropriately at the right time and remain changed until otherwise specified?

- Does your treatment of various issues or scenarios align throughout the book?

- Is there anything you mention at some point in your introduction or thesis that immediately disappears?

Essentially, you want to read through your book and not once think, "Wait, what happened to ___." Whether that blank is filled by an important historical reference, a character name, a recognizable tattoo, a dog, an interviewee, a significant resource, or a portion of your argument, don't let it dangle.

So how do you clean it up? Start with evaluation. Do you really need that thing that fills the blank to exist in the first place? What type of effort in the form of rewrites will be needed to re-establish consistency? While you may find that you can get rid of the offending disagreeable detail, it may be salvageable. You may, in fact, find that taking the time to do some pretty sizable rewrites to explain the inconsistency will not only eliminate confusion but bolster your work altogether. Nearly every writer has had a cringe-worthy moment where they discovered a major boo-boo or blunder, only to write it into the text with great success.

Once you've got a thorough and complete text without any strange wandering threads that lead nowhere, it's time to address the language and grammar. If you're using a word processing program, you'll likely have minimal typos, unless you happen to make typos that actually make sense. I really need to send my editors a fruit basket at some point, because they have caught me in the act of things that legitimately don't make sense. After all, Google Docs autocorrected my typos to something similar but not right. You'll want to find those before you release your book to the outside world. Even if you never intend your text to see wide distribution, you do want to avoid hearing every person who does read the book say "Did you know that on page 113, you used the word 'lighting' instead of 'lightning?'" And yes, that is a real example from my own career-- the error appeared in a commemorative handbook for a one-time event, and I may never recover.

At this point, you have uncovered and corrected all glaring errors and omissions. If this is a low-stakes project, you may wish to press forward and pursue distribution of your project now, whether that means printing up booklets for your friends or family or sending off a file to your loved ones. However, if you want to make a big splash with your first book, it's time to call in an outside party to read and evaluate your text. Sounds scary? It's absolutely terrifying, at least the first few times. But having a beta reader or editing team tear your book to bits is far less dehumanizing than reading negative reviews. Trust me.

The Importance of Outside Readers

If you're concerned about letting other people read your work, imagine how I'm feeling right now. I'm writing a chapter about editing that will be edited by my long-suffering editors. Talk about working under pressure!

The truth of the matter is that I, personally, am thrilled when my work goes off to editors and beta readers. I feel like I write in a vacuum, typing out things that only I might ever want to read, so having a clean-up crew to make what I write suitable for public consumption is a major relief to me. In fact, if a manuscript comes back without being shredded, redlined, and annotated, I become paranoid that I've done something wrong.

The purpose of an editor is to catch what you've missed. An ideal editor should have a strong background in language and grammar, and understand the various current formats for both fiction and nonfiction pieces. I went to school in the 1980s. The styles we used back then are long gone, and the grammar guides that led to my high marks in literature and writing are now laughably out of date. I try to keep up, but then I throw out a super-casual, candid, conversational book like this one, and my poor editors suffer trying to make it fit a format. And I would like to note that I am very, very sorry for their suffering, even though they'll likely remove one of those "very" for being redundant.

Beta readers, on the other hand, are there to make sure your text works. They can provide editing and formatting corrections as necessary, but the primary goal of a beta reader is to make sure that the book works before anyone sees it. Much like a trusted friend evaluating your hair, makeup, and outfit before you leave the house for an important shindig, the beta reader ensures your slip isn't showing and there isn't lipstick on your teeth, metaphorically speaking.

The purpose of an editor or beta reader is to approach your book objectively, without any bias or preconceived notion. Therefore, you may not want a close friend, housemate, or partner to be your first reader, unless they are very good at separating the art from the artist. What I mean by that is this: someone who knows you very well will know your tone of voice, how you communicate, and even the subconscious nuances of the way you speak and think. They'll read your book in your voice, which will be beneficial for them, but not every reader will have that same understanding of your style.

If an editor or beta reader has done a very thorough job, they'll share their own insight into what they like about your book, and what didn't work for them. I strongly encourage you to consider this information. With a few exceptions, they aren't sharing their thoughts and recommendations to be mean, but rather because they have discovered opportunities for making your book even stronger. Let your soul and your ego rest peacefully, knowing that this isn't an attack, but rather an invitation from a like-minded friend to make things even better than they are.

It is very easy, as a writer, to write from your own point of view and understanding about a topic. Unfortunately, that makes assumptions about what the reader already knows and understands. Very rarely are these things universal. Therefore, when an editor or beta reader points out that the jump from point to point doesn't make sense, don't bother thinking "No one understands me as a writer," but rather, "What can I do to make this clearer to my audience?" Remember that you're trying to create a clear picture of your intentions, regardless of whether you're writing fiction or nonfiction. Clarity is the best way to get your reader on board, so if those who are reading the book are having trouble following, it doesn't mean you're a horrible writer, but merely that you have some explaining to do.

I realize that can be a big jolt to the ego, especially when you've tried your best and it's your first effort. But before you begin licking your wounds and avowing you'll never write again, pause for a moment and really read the comments you've received from your outside reader. It is very possible that they simply weren't the right readers for the assignment. It is also possible that they headed into it with a very different concept of what they were supposed to be doing. Any editor or beta reader worth their salt will leave a slew of comments and feedback about your work. You'll be able to tell from reading them not only what they objectively thought, but what they expected from your work, as well. Sometimes-- however unintentional it may be-- what they want your book to be will differ from what's on the page, which will lead to a whole avalanche of misunderstanding and lack of appreciation.

One way to mitigate this is to do a trial run with your outside reader. Send them a few pages. A chapter. See what they do with it. If they come back to you with feedback that makes sense, then you've got a good match, and you should run with it. Let them have at it and build a better book. Alternatively, if they clearly missed the point of the assignment, perhaps they should wait for the final product. They may be wonderful, perfectly intelligent people, but just as you wouldn't want to listen to an entire album in a musical style you loathe, forcing someone to read a book they just don't get is equally unfair, and no one will benefit from it. While you want your book to have the greatest appeal possible, truly nothing in this world is beloved by all... not even cheese.

My last piece of advice when it comes to working with editors, beta readers, and outside parties of all kinds is this: You don't always have to take their advice. At the end of the day, this is your book, filled with your ideas, research, time, energy, and sense of humor. At some point, you will need to decide for and by yourself that the book you have created is exactly the product you intended in the first place.

And that part is tough enough that it gets its own chapter.

When to Call It "Done"

When I was a young person, studying writing at school, I hated what our professor called "rewind weeks." That week, instead of submitting a brand-new piece for peer review and group discussion, we were to take a previous piece and make it new again. Hardly anyone liked it. One fellow, in particular, would do something delightfully subservient, like change a single character's appearance in a way that really didn't matter to the context of the story and leave everything else the same. One writer enjoyed rewriting his work so that the letter "e" wouldn't appear anywhere in the text. The rest of us, however, begrudgingly leafed through our portfolio to figure out what we could unenthusiastically turn into a new piece.

But here's the thing: we were all missing the point of the exercise. The whole reason why we were doing this was to drill home the lesson that any piece you write is going to be a reflection of who, where, what, and how you were at the time you wrote it. When you do massive revisions, it's usually because the version of yourself reading the book is markedly different from the person who wrote it in the first place. While you're welcome to do that, you need to know that you aren't required to do so.

Sometimes, it's best to just let a piece be. There have been many times when writers look at something and say, "That's crap. I'll have the editors deal with it," again, with apologies to my editors. But then the editors take a look at it and feel that it isn't crap at all. That's because we're our own worst critics, and we won't let things leave our grasp while we can still control everything about them. Sounds psychologically deep, but many of us are hardwired to be absolute control monsters, and that's okay.

Letting go of a manuscript is hard. I genuinely cried the first time I submitted a final draft, as I mentioned before. I was equal parts proud of myself, relieved that the process was done, and terrified that I had just unleashed a bunch of garbage on the literary community. The truth is that most of the things that are written will be sublimely enjoyed by many people, while others just don't care for it very much… just like cheese.

This does not mean you're a failure. Negative feedback and destructive criticism have nothing to do with you or your talents. If someone truly cares, they'll leave you constructive feedback and notes that can help you build upon themselves. Otherwise, they're just miserable people who want the world to know they've had an awful time.

Think of your favorite musical artist. Do you know how many people hate their work? Bach, Beethoven, The Beatles, Beck... for each of these artists there is someone out there who hates everything they've done with a passion so deep they could choke on it. But that doesn't mean they aren't talented and don't deserve their careers. It means there's someone who just doesn't like them.

So, when you receive harsh words about your book-- whether they're from someone else or your own brain-- let it go. It's one book in a vast universe of books. It's one literary experience. At some point, you have to stop picking at it and just let it live the way it was intended.

That doesn't mean you have to completely tune out any feedback about the book. If something is universally confusing, then it might need some patient tinkering. But if people just don't like it, then they can donate it or put it in a garage sale. Everyone in this world has albums, movies, books, and even clothing that they once loved, but now realize they bought in error. The world keeps turning.

Earlier in this book, I mentioned how you do need to do some things for readers, such as make an intelligible book. That courtesy does not extend to making sure they absolutely adore the book. At the dawn of my career, I edited and beta read for a person whose books were truly appalling to me. His characters were racist, there was a sexual assault of some kind in each chapter, and I simply couldn't follow the plot lines at all because I was so emotionally triggered. I came to realize that I was just not the best beta reader for his books, and we parted ways amicably. Guess who's working with a team to develop his work for television. Everything has an audience. Don't find inspiration in the harsh words of the naysayers; grow with those who already know you're capable.

So, now that you've learned that you can always change things and no one's going to like everything anyway, including yourself, that leaves the question that started this chapter: How do you know when your book is done?

The very textbook, fact-based answer is that your book is done once you've reached a point where you're confident that it fully reflects all of the intentions you outlined in your pre-work. Though things changed during the pre-work and the writing itself, the general idea of writing a decent book on a specific topic should still be the bullseye you've been aiming for all along. If each page makes sense and contributes something to the overall book and reader experience, then you're done. Save file. Submit. Print. Whatever you plan to do with your completed book, now is the time to do it. Have a toast, call your friends, cry... whatever it takes to release all of the emotions and stress you've built along the road.

The esoteric version of this is that you'll simply know. Sometimes, you'll get through a round of edits and just know that your book is ready to fly. Alternatively, you'll be so sick of looking at it that you don't care if it flops, as long as it gets off of your desktop. Realistically, the logic behind these feelings is the knowledge within yourself that there is simply nothing else you can do to make the book any more ready than it is at that moment. But the romantic notion of understanding your book on a spiritual level is a bit more fun than really digging into the psychology of it.

If you are going to publish your book on a public level, beyond distribution to your inner circle, this is not the end of the line. You can certainly cheer, cry, and celebrate, but there may still be some work to be done on your end. Read on to determine how-- and if-- you want your book to see the light of day.

A BRIEF WORD ABOUT PUBLISHING

Years ago, publishing a piece meant sending it off to be printed in a bound book format with shiny covers and real pages that could be rudely dog-eared. With the advent of the household printer, it became easier to print off entire pieces without them ever passing the threshold, though it's difficult to say that using a household printer was ever "easy." Paper jams, impossible toner levels, and the cost of printer paper made it a less than enjoyable process, but nonetheless, one anyone with the right equipment could complete.

Today, there are many paths to publication on a variety of scales. The difficulty, stress, and rewards for each method are very different and should be thoroughly considered before throwing all of your proverbial eggs in one proverbial basket.

Each of the methods for getting published that I'll mention is worthy of its own book, but I'm going to skim over each for now. There are several reasons for this. First, I don't want anyone to feel that publishing is mandatory. Writing for pleasure is still very much a real thing, and I want anyone attempting to write a book to feel like this can be our little secret. Next, the publishing world is so volatile, that I couldn't possibly do it justice without writing a lengthy volume. Furthermore, the methods are constantly changing and may be different from location to location, person to person, or website to website. It's a very nuanced business, so rather than provide you with any details that might be inaccurate, I'll instead give you the basics and point you in the direction of more authoritative information.

Ghost Writing

Ghostwriting is a term used to describe a situation where one party hires another party to write about a particular topic on their behalf. Many people are looking for ghostwriters, especially those looking for someone to capture in the written word their own advice or life story. As a new writer, this can be beneficial because someone else is guiding you, and that dangling paycheck just beyond the deadline can be a great incentive... as long as you're confident that you can follow through with the commitment.

Pros:

- All you have to do is write and edit

- No politics, no agents

- You'll likely get paid

- If the book tanks, no one knows it was you who wrote it

Cons:

- You usually do not get to choose the topic

- The person requesting the writing may have very specific requirements, including a deadline

- No commission

- If the book performs extremely well, no one knows it was you who wrote it

Self-Publishing

There are many venues out there for self-publishing your book, so take the time to explore your options to find the best fit for you and your goals. In this method of publication, you hire editors and designers to format your book, then submit it for publication through a business that strictly prints your book to order. Many publication venues have a minimum number of physical books they'll print at a time, but self-published eBooks are extremely popular.

Pros:

- You can print anything anytime

- You don't have to print millions of copies

- You can earn a commission, depending on the distribution method or site you use

- You can make changes to your book at any time since they are printed to order. Just make sure you're using the latest file for future publications

Cons:
- You'll need to have design skills, or higher someone to ensure it's formatted correctly for publishing or eBook distribution

- You will not see your face smiling back at you from a book jacket in the window of a bookstore

- You don't commission unless it sells. All marketing and promotion is up to you

- You will need to pay for each copy that is produced, which means you may lose money at first

Finding an Agent/Publisher

Not for the faint of heart or those with low to moderate self-esteem. This is the most political version of getting your work published, but if you're very much interested in becoming a famous author, you'll want to consider finding an agent.

In this model, you send your book to agents who are looking for new material. Agents work on commission; therefore, it is in the best interest of each agent to only take on clients they believe they can sell. If an agent does not believe they can sell your book, they will reject it. Rejection hurts, but it's not personal.

Once you find an agent, the agent will pitch your book to a variety of publishing houses. Again, they will only accept your work if they think they can profit from it. If they don't think there's money in your book, they will reject it.

Eventually, your book will be published. You will be paid royalties, which are a percentage of the profit of your book. Your book will need to sell so many copies to pay for its own publishing, so you will only get paid after your book has "earned out," or paid for itself.

Pros:
- You don't have to pay to publish your own work

- You may be asked to produce multiple books

- Being signed by a publisher is a big deal with significant prestige and honor

- You won't have to do any of the hustling, like marketing, printing, ordering, and design

Cons:

- You may have to relinquish creative control. Always review your contract in detail

- You may be rejected many times before you finally find an agent and publisher

- Your contract may limit your rights to your original work

- You may be forced to do press and signings (which might be a pro if you're into that sort of thing!)

Publishing your work is often a strange juxtaposition of guts and glory. I've included some resources to help you dig further into any options that might sound ideal for you and your goals for your freshly written book.

CONCLUSION

So, there you go. That's how you do it. Go write a book.

At this point, you may still feel like you don't entirely know "how" to write a book. I wish I could say that there's a step-by-step process that's super easy to follow and absolutely fail-proof, but there's really not.

Avid readers may recall the journey of a girl named Dorothy Gale along a certain Yellow Brick Road. She had guidance along the way, but there was quite a bit that she had to figure out on her own. At the risk of throwing yet another analogy on the heap, writing a book is a very similar exercise in endurance and perseverance. If you have a general idea of where you're headed and a destination or goal in mind, you'll be very well prepared to handle any bumps in the road that might head your way, whether you realize it or not.

You might feel right now that I haven't possibly addressed every single step, every possible problem or pratfall, and how to get out of it. In fact, I have. Most of the obstacles that try us during the process of writing our first books come from the enemy within us. More than anything, novice writers are typically tripped up and dissuaded from completing big projects because they feel it would be a waste of time. They aren't good enough to write a book. They started a book once, but they lost interest in it. They decided they "sounded dumb," so they gave up. When I ask people how their books are going, and they are not going well at all, these are the types of answers I receive.

What I hope I have impressed upon you, more than anything else, is that you have the power within you to get past these obstacles. Writing a book takes a lot of time, which is why I warned you of that right from the get-out. Time, energy, and a sense of humor are all required to make it through the process of writing a book, whether it's your first or your 101st effort.

You will spend a lot of time writing a book, but whether that time is truly "wasted" is for you to decide. Human beings are very good at finding new and exciting ways to waste time, and frankly, if you felt like you got something from it, emotionally, spiritually, mentally, physically, educationally, or what-have-you, then my personal view is that your time was not "wasted." It was used in an atypical way to provide you with personal enrichment.

As far as whether you're "good enough?" By now, you should be aware that we are all simultaneously good enough and not good enough. Some readers will love it. Some will hate it. The majority of readers will think it's fine and have no major feelings one way or the other about it.

At the beginning of the book, we talked about maintaining realistic expectations for books, and figuring out why we wanted to write them in the first place. Aligning our priorities mentally and emotionally when it comes to undertaking an entire tome is directly related to the level of energy we put into getting the task done. Aim higher than you need to, and you'll put undue pressure on yourself, struggling to write a book and ultimately feeling like you've "failed," which is false. You'll put too much energy in too fast and burn out when you discover the process can take a miserable amount of time and more than basic enthusiasm. As I said then, writing a best seller is a remarkable goal, but don't register for the marathon without jogging a few steps first. You are good enough; you just need to set yourself up to succeed.

And then that sense of humor. At some point, everyone seems to feel like they "sound dumb." I would absolutely love to read more psychological and sociological studies examining why those in creative fields doubt their own abilities and intelligence. In the meantime, I can only speculate and recommend you meditate on these concepts to see if they can help you break through some mental blockages of your own.

When you write, especially if you've never written before, you're using your mind and your body in new ways. It's all very unfamiliar, and sometimes, if you stare at a page or a word too long, you stop recognizing it. Don't let your brain play games with your spirit. A sense of humor will get you far in the writing process.

When you find yourself feeling ignorant or start having negative thoughts about your capabilities, take a break. Go do some research to validate yourself. Read a book by an author you admire. Some writers recommend reading an author in your genre, but I find that leads me down a path of temptation to compare myself to the other author. Let your brain find inspiration without dysfunction-- that is, fill your brain with information that will reignite your passion to pursue this endeavor, without feeding into any negative self-talk.

Always do the pre-work. As time goes by, and you gain more experience, you may find this part of the process going more and more smoothly. After a while, it starts to feel less like work and more like "the fun part." Really let yourself soar when it comes to dreaming up your book, especially in the very first few moments of making it real. Start really, really big, and then let yourself understand your book and where it really needs to go in order to make yourself clear.

In fact, allow yourself to suspend disbelief a bit in these first few days of getting to know your book. I like to really immerse myself in whatever I'm writing about. If it's a particular brand of car, for example, I'll look at pictures, read the history of the manufacturer, and even drive past a dealership lot if I can. When I'm writing a fiction piece, I like to really imagine who each character is. Don't give them arbitrary descriptions; instead, think about how they wear their hair (if they have hair). What's their posture like? How do they move? What do their facial expressions look like? It sounds a little strange at first, but consider how your belief in this new reality that you're creating will help the reader ease more swiftly into your newfound world.

When you finally feel ready to sit down and write, make sure you are really prepared to commit to this undertaking. You're going to feel uncomfortable in every imaginable sense of the word, at least for the first few sessions. Are you prepared to break through the agony to pursue the ecstasies of writing?

Rather than arming you with a gimmick that claims to help newcomers write better, I'm furnishing you with certain truths and expectations that aren't discussed widely, though I'm not sure why the secrecy is so well-maintained. Whenever I mention through the introduction that I'm a writer, this detail is more and more frequently met with a self-deprecating joke about how the other party is "practically illiterate," or something along those lines. While I would absolutely love to be validated in my suspicions that I am the most talented beast walking this planet, deep down inside, I know that's not true.

Furthermore, it makes me very sad that so many people have had their confidence completely squelched when it comes to doing something creative. Why are standards so high that no one can simply dabble in art, music, crafting, cooking, or writing without being extremely good at it? You haven't "tried to write a book" if you got three sentences in and decided you were a failure. You weren't. You got overwhelmed. You psyched yourself out. You chose to quit before you had to admit it was uncomfortable and you weren't sure how to deal with that discomfort.

The writing process is truly unlike anything else. While there is some order to things, it's not an exact science, except for some forms of nonfiction. If you prefer detailed instructions, you need to figure them out yourself. Just like the road trip from Seattle to Boca, there are a vast quantity of possible routes. But don't let that be your reason for never making the trip. Maps were made by people taking the trip and figuring out where to go. You'll need to make your own map the first time you make this particular journey, and that can certainly be overwhelming. But think how much more fun the next road trip will be, now that you know the best route.

If anything, I want you to feel empowered by this book to take the plunge and make it through the writing process. You certainly won't arrive at the end unscathed, but I hope that the previous pages of text have helped you understand some of the perils that await along the path. The creative process is all about exploration and experimentation, which can be utterly terrifying for those who have never dabbled in these particular areas. Take comfort in knowing that it doesn't go smoothly for anyone.

Press forward, and then press forward again. Dismiss criticism and consider constructive critique, even that which comes from your own mind.

For those who intend to distribute your book, keep in mind the benefits and things to be wary of when it comes to editing. Don't just worry about editors and beta readers; think about yourself and your relentless desire to pick things to bits *ad nauseam*. Learn when to make peace with, not pieces of your book. Find a way to let go and let it fly.

So how do you feel now? Ready to write a book? Take it one step at a time. When you get overwhelmed, pause yourself. Always maintain forward momentum. Don't get inside your own head.

Above all: Revel in every moment of the creative process. Even the not-so-lovely ones.

Good luck. May your fingers be swift and your muse always close at hand!

RESOURCES

T he following resources are intended to help inspire and excite you as a new writer. All sources have been credited where possible. Please don't consider the inclusion of any of these links as endorsements or partnerships; we aren't getting paid for sharing them, either. Consider this your friendly author friend sharing with you some interesting things that help them with this process.

The following sections outline all of the things you were promised in the main text, and then some. I've included a variety of resources that will help you get out of sticky situations and guide you through some organizational strategies, all to keep that forward momentum and productivity rolling.

Enjoy at your own leisure, and remember, truly nothing in this world is beloved by all... not even cheese. I've made it a point to include a few different varieties of each resource, but if none of these suits your particular methods, use this as a launchpad for discovering your own way!

Writing Exercises

Writing truly is an exercise for the mind, spirit, and body. From time to time, you may find yourself lacking in whatever mojo gets the creative juices flowing. When that happens, consider a writing exercise or two to help you navigate back to a space where imagination is more possible and thoughts are more organized. I've included many different types of writing exercises, neither of which is exclusively intended for writers of fiction or nonfiction. Basically, any time you find yourself falling off track, feel free to employ one of these exercises to help you find the way back to the path.

Eventually, you'll feel your flow return. If not, choose a different writing exercise, move on to brain cleansers, or grab a cup of tea and come back to it.

This is not a comprehensive list of exercises. These are just a few examples that I use in my own work. Feel free to look up even more exercises to help your imagination soar.

1. "Narrate Your Day." This one is fun because you don't even have to write anything down. This exercise is best in situations where you just can't get the words to appear, and you feel like you can't remember how to write.

To narrate your day, explain to yourself what you're doing at the moment. If you're a bit low on verbs at the moment, you can describe your surroundings. Don't think too much about it, just start describing:

"I sit perpendicular to a window. On my desk, which was once tragically painted white, a monitor glows bright white in the quickly dimming room."

"I was brushing my teeth. There was not enough toothpaste on the brush, but I lacked the concern to do anything about it. With my luck, I'd drop the toothbrush in the toilet if I tried to change anything about the situation. Best to let it ride."

Start with something obvious and real. Expand upon it. Add description. Give it life. Repeat.

1. "This Is My..." *This* is another description exercise. I like to use this one when I'm trying to set a scene, bring a character to life, or really drive home a particular piece of evidence, but I seem to have forgotten all of my words.

For this exercise, choose an object. Any object, as long as you can actually see it and experience it in person at this exact moment. Start with the words "This is my," followed by the name of the object. Then describe it. Don't worry about it making sense right away. Just start writing out your description, then keep going until you run out of things to say about it. Then keep going. Eventually, you will run out of things to say about your trinket or geejaw, but keep pushing yourself to say more, whether that means adding more adjectives and adverbs, or including its significance in this universe.

1. "I Read the News Today, Oh Boy." I like this one when I'm having trouble making connections happen or when I need to get over my own ego. You'll need some form of physical media that includes pictures and words, such as a newspaper, magazine, brochure, or catalog.

Find a picture of a person. That's your protagonist. Find another picture of a person. That's your antagonist. Find a sentence that includes an action verb, like "robbed a bank," or "receives a medal of honor." Write a little story in which those two people do the thing. Remember this is just garbage, and write off the head. Excuse typos. Ignore grammar. Freestyle it. Feign shock and surprise when it turns out pretty good and definitely worth putting a little more effort into developing. Finish one book before you start another.

1. "Get Out." This is a bit of more traditional journaling, with a tad bit of therapy attached. Basically, you'll free-write your way to mental freedom. Prepare a blank page. Close your eyes. Write. Every thought, make it come out. Think of it as clearing your cache.

Prompts

Many people use the terms "writing exercises" and "writing prompts" interchangeably. This isn't incorrect, but for the purpose of this book, I'm using "prompts" to describe mechanisms for getting unstuck when you've found yourself in a rut.

Use these prompts to help you redirect and refocus when you feel like you're repeating yourself, not saying enough, or "sounding dumb." Reach out and grab onto these prompts like a carrot on a stick- they can help pull you to safety!

1. Select a specific person in your life, and tell them what comes next. You can actually do this, or perform this exercise mentally. For example, "Ok, Meemaw, so after our hero goes to the castle, there's going to be a dragon, right? And the dragon is not going to see our hero, because... because... because he's under a sleeping spell!"

2. Stop acting like you're writing, and act like you're talking to someone. I strongly recommend you make a note to yourself in your writing journal about the exact page you were on when you implemented this prompt because things might get a little weird. Write exactly like you would speak, even if that includes curse words or colloquialisms, song lyrics, or whatever. You will inevitably find yourself naturally "talking" your way back into the book's original format.

3. Look up synonyms. This may sound strange, but looking at words can sometimes reignite a mind that's been simmering on low for too long. I once submitted an article for publication thinking I'd done a good job. The editor asked me if I had realized I used the word "influence" ten times in a single paragraph, and that two paragraphs covered the same information in different manners. My brain had clearly been stagnant. Looking up other words helped me diversify my thinking

process and move forward meaningfully.

4. Ask yourself "Why". Children are very good at asking why things are the way they are, but adults tend to lose this sense of wonder. When you find yourself stumbling around, trying in vain to describe something or some piece of data, stop wandering and ask "Why?"

- Why did this happen?

- Why do I need to know this?

- Why am I explaining this now?

- Why does the reader care?

Character Map Examples

For my fiction-writing friends, here are a few samples and templates to help you organize your characters. As discussed earlier, the purpose of a character map is to keep you from forgetting who is who and who does what. Additionally, a character map can help you discover more and more interesting traits regarding your characters. Each of these examples is quite different, so take a look, give each a try, and decide what you need to keep the citizens of your new world in line.

This particular form allows you to truly discover who your characters are as human beings. This is possibly the most detailed version I've found yet: http://www.epiguide.com/ep101/writing/charchart.html

Some of the ins and outs of character mapping techniques, along with great examples: https://www.thenovelry.com/blog/character-map

Here's a technique that involves a family-tree style map, as well as tips on organizing their biographies:

http://writeonsisters.com/writing-craft/6-easy-steps-to-great-character-mapping/This link leads to an online shop for teachers to share and sell character map templates. The prices are quite reasonable, especially for a resource you'll enjoy many times over!

https://www.teacherspayteachers.com/Browse/Search:character%20map%20template

Plot Outline Examples

If you do a simple search for "plot outlines" or "plot diagrams," you'll more than likely find a drawing of a line that rises slowly, reaches a peak, and then plummets swiftly. This drawing is the simplest explanation for a plot. As a writer, you'll find that your plot more greatly resembles a distressed spider's web than a beautiful single line; however, I cannot argue that the simplest templates get the job done. Here are a few examples of plot outlines to help you get your own plot details situated.

This is obviously an example of someone's personal template, and I very much like the style and simplicity of it. If you're in the early stages of figuring out actions and reactions, give a sample like this a try.

https://karcherry.files.wordpress.com/2013/07/plot-outline1.jpg

This version is very handy for those who have multiple questions to answer throughout the course of your book. Very rarely is our hero focused on just one thing at a time. An outline like this will help you reveal and map the course of each source of strife.

https://diymfa.com/writing/mapping-out-your-story

This link leads to several different types of plot outline templates. I like #5 in particular, because that looks a lot like my own plot outlines. If you're not sure which version of a plot outline would best stimulate your brain, take a cruise through the examples here to try a few different options.

https://templatelab.com/story-outline/

And since we've used her works as an example several times, I thought it might be interesting to share with you how author J.K. Rowling put together the *Harry Potter* books. This article includes the handwritten plot outline for chapters 13–24 of *Harry Potter and the Order of the Phoenix.* Notice how she tracks all of the simultaneously existing storylines on the horizontal, then fills in the necessary developments to each story on the vertical, chapter by chapter.

http://blog.paperblanks.com/2013/05/j-k-rowling-book-outline/

Nonfiction Outline Examples

Nonfiction works also require significant prework, as we discovered in the second section of this book. The purpose of an outline is to help you figure out how to get from one important point in your discussion to another. You can use the outline to help you set the tone or to help you remember key resources or quotes to help drive your discourse forward.

In the interest of showing my own work, here's my own outline for this book. Basically, I started with the concept of "How to Write a Book." Then I quite literally went stream of consciousness for the outline so that I could nail down what I wanted to share. I'm sure you'll be able to spot the differences and similarities.

https://docs.google.com/document/d/1Pbv1obA4W_v_IlQYRMHP8VArTHyj-upb9 4CW1dq2474/edit?usp=sharing

As you can see, my method most reflects the standard outline method, also presented here.

https://writenonfictionnow.com/outlining-first-time-self-published-authors/

One extra tidbit I'd like to add is that, if you are using quotes or specific sections of resources, it is very helpful to include a link for or the basic bibliographic information for that quote or resource in your outline so you don't struggle to find it later.

Here is the world-famous Scrivener outline method. This writer provides a video as well as an explanation as to how the method works for her, and some tips and tricks for using it.

https://authorbasics.com/using-scrivener-outline-non-fiction-book/

There are a few different samples included in this link for different types of nonfiction. If you're writing a book that isn't a simple wander through points to be made and discussions to be had, this link will help you figure out a creative and enjoyable flow of thoughts for your audience.

https://laptrinhx.com/news/how-to-write-a-nonfiction-book-free-chapter-outlining-te mplates-oAZ8D5e/

Nonfiction Table Of Content Examples

My editors will be the first people to tell you that my inclusion of this topic is purely hypocritical since I really don't follow any particular format or template when I'm writing for myself. I abandoned the idea of following a format during my first year of copywriting when I discovered that every client has developed their own formatting, and it's best to forget what you were taught in school and do what the person with the money wants. However, as a new writer who has not been subjected to years of memorizing the nuances of various formats only to have them change before you can put them to use, you likely would like some help with formatting.

The following are sites that provide templates for creating a TOC for your nonfiction masterpiece.

This link includes a variety of formats and templates, ranging from the highly stylistic to the very structured. Remember that you are using the TOC to help you organize and stay on track, and choose a version that is right for the task.

https://www.template.net/business/word-templates/table-of-contents/

I like this guide from Sam Houston University (again, I have no affiliation with them; I simply like this link) because it demonstrates the full scholarly version of the table of contents, which you will note I personally have completely disregarded. If you are going to be shopping your work to a publisher, you'll most likely need to write this more formal APA version of a TOC in your final draft before shipping it off...

https://shsulibraryguides.org/thesisguide/tableofcontents

...unless you're using the Chicago style, in which case, you'll want to click on this link, instead.

https://www.scientific-editing.info/blog/chicago-table-of-contents/

Types of Nonfiction Organization / Formats

If you just saw the words "APA" and "Chicago" in the section above and had a mild wave of anxiety pass over you because you don't know what those are, here they are. As mentioned in the chapter regarding the organization or format of your piece, there are quite a few different methods, none of which are super important unless you're looking to publish your piece or place it under formal review. Again, I'm a very naughty writer who has used a mish-mash of styles for this book, but it's pretty clear by now that this is a very casual, candid piece, and not a scholarly work.

Check out the following links, and decide which feels more natural for you. If you are submitting your work for publishing or review, double-check with the publisher regarding their exact formatting requirements.

APA: American Psychological Association. Yes, really. Their preferred publishing format has been adopted across the writing community for scholarly pieces.

https://apastyle.apa.org/

Chicago: Developed in 1906 by the University of Chicago Press, this style is usually associated with topics surrounding business, arts, history, and humanities.

https://www.chicagomanualofstyle.org/home.html

MLA: The Modern Language Association developed this format in 1833, and it's changed several times since then. Currently, in their 9th edition, MLA sells handbooks, though some rules and tips are provided free of charge online. This style is generally applied to studies of language, culture, and human interest, and is very popular with college professors.

https://style.mla.org/mla-format

MECE: This is not a publication format, but rather an organizational formatting option. It's somewhat controversial; however, for those who tend to go off on stream-of-consciousness tangents when writing, it can help provide a little discipline when organizing your nonfiction piece.

https://www.caseinterview.com/mece

Desk Exercises

Writing is hard on the body as well as the mind, especially if you're not used to sitting down and wiggling your fingers to make words appear for hours at a time. You may find your back, posterior, legs, hips, arms, and fingers aching after your first few sessions.

Additionally, a stagnant body can lead to a bored mind, which is not helpful when you're trying to be creative. Get up and move every 30 minutes or so, or when you find yourself at a loss for words.

In reading these links, please note that I am not a doctor, and nothing I write should be considered medical advice. Always address discomfort with a trained physician.

This link offers loads of exercises you can do without leaving your desk, though you should definitely leave your desk every once in a while!

https://www.healthline.com/health/fitness/office-exercises

You're going to have to get up from your desk to do these exercises, but you'll be glad you did:

https://yogawithadriene.com/yoga-for-writers/

Here are some hand and wrist exercises to help you keep limber in between sessions:

https://www.webmd.com/osteoarthritis/ss/slideshow-hand-finger-exercises

This link provides some excellent options for getting your cardio in while psychologically chained to your writing. Plus, it uses the term "Deskercise," which I adore.

https://greatist.com/fitness/deskercise-33-ways-exercise-work

Brain Cleansers

Brain cleansers are exercises for your mind and emotions. Writing can be draining, especially if you're very passionate about what you're writing or simply feeling stressed by any part of the process. Stress is normal and can be good, but too much leads to writer's block, headaches, or worse-- quitting.

If you feel yourself getting overwhelmed, here are a few things you can do to chill out and get back on task.

Yoga Nidra:

Yoga Nidra is an excellent relaxation and centering technique that allows you to bring awareness to each part of your body individually. A form of meditation that can reorganize a frazzled brain, it can also bring your brain into a state of restfulness without that post-nap grogginess.

I don't know this person or have any affiliation with their YouTube channel, but I do appreciate the variety of practices offered here.

https://www.youtube.com/c/SarovaraYoga

For those who would like to learn more about the practice, a colleague of mine has written a book on the topic that gives a great introduction. This person I do know, but I'm not getting any kickbacks for mentioning her book:

https://www.amazon.com/Nidra-Yoga-beginners-increase-productivity-ebook/dp/B07 ZQR81PT/ref=tmm_kin_swatch_0?_encoding=UTF8&qid=1635527242&sr=8-1

Games:

Depending on where your stress levels have taken you, you might prefer playing a game to help you return to your regular functional self. These games have been recommended for those looking to tune back into themselves and leave the chaos behind.

https://www.self.com/story/free-mobile-games

These, on the other hand, will spark greater activity in the brain.

https://www.lifehack.org/articles/technology/11-brain-training-apps-train-your-mind-and-improve-memory.html

Breathing Exercises:

You may not connect breathing with your brain, but when the thoughts stop and your heart starts racing, focusing on your breath can restore harmony in your body.

https://www.uofmhealth.org/health-library/uz2255

https://www.youtube.com/watch?v=MlaSf1D9tbA
https://yogawithadriene.com/free-yoga-videos/pranayama/

How to Get Published

Since I glossed over this topic earlier, I've included a few helpful resources to help guide you further along with the various publication options mentioned earlier.

Ghostwriting:

The steps and tricks you'll need to keep in mind when getting started as a ghostwriter

https://thewritelife.com/how-to-become-a-ghostwriter/

Some things to consider before you take the plunge

https://theregalwriter.com/2020/10/09/know-the-pros-and-cons-of-ghostwriting/

Self-publishing:

Where you can go to get your book self-published

https://selfpublishing.com/self-publishing-companies/

Amazon's guide to self-publishing

https://kdp.amazon.com/en_US/

How to get started with the process, and know whether it's ideal for you

https://knliterary.com/how-to-self-publish-a-book/

Traditional publishing:

This guide provides very detailed and solid information on both self and traditional publishing

https://writersdigestshop.com/pages/how-to-publish-a-book-an-overview-of-traditional-self-publishing

This guide includes real authors talking about the process and the various considerations of traditional publishing

https://getpublished.penguin.co.uk/

This article includes links to some common resources for finding and wooing a literary agent

https://shutupwrite.com/how-to-find-a-literary-agent/

Communities for New Writers

For those looking for support, encouragement, critique, or validation, here are some links to online forums or communities dedicated to new writers. I cannot speak for the overall quality or politeness of all communities, so I encourage you to read and lurk a bit before you start joining in the discussion. Like all groups of people, some will be ideal for you, and others will not. Proceed at your own risk.

Writing Forums: https://www.writingforums.com/

She Writes: https://www.shewrites.com/

NaNoWriMo: https://nanowrimo.org/

Critique Circle: https://new.critiquecircle.com/landing

Go forth, be bold, and write a book!

Non-Fiction for Newbies

How to Write a Factual Book and Actually Kind of Enjoy It

Lauren Bingham

Contents

INTRODUCTION

"But basically, you just tell everybody whatever happened. What was said? What was done? It's all right there. You don't need to make anything up. It's got to be way easier than writing a story where you have to make up a magical land and draw maps and invent languages and whatever."

My friend was trying to understand why I was frazzled after doing a final editing push with a 30,000-word nonfiction piece. I'm not even sure "frazzled" is the best word to use. I love my job, but there's this adrenaline rush that comes at the end of a book, then the tension of the editing tap dance, and once it's all said and done, you choose the cover for your book and fall into a sort of fugue state or stupor.

It was this state of mind that inspired my response of "Whaa...? No, but you... it doesn't just happen. You have to write it."

My friend nodded sympathetically. "There, there," he said, reaching across the cafe table to pat my hand lovingly. "Let's just get you a yummy dessert with some chocolate in it."

The healing properties of chocolate did, in fact, revive me, and I was able to explain some of the challenges of writing nonfiction in actual words and concepts. Eventually, I was able to convince him that the rumors were not true: writing nonfiction is just as hard, and in some ways even harder, than writing fiction pieces.

Nonfiction indeed comes from a place of reality. It may be spun, twisted, distorted, edited, or even censored, but somewhere in there is a real person, place, or situation. The reader is drawn to these books because they want to read about something very specific and very real that has touched them in some way. For example, you're likely reading this book because you are interested in the process behind writing nonfiction books.

Writing about reality is an art form. Let's take a look at the start of this book, and my retelling of my encounter with a friend. That really happened. We could consider this as part of a longer autobiographical piece or memoir, depending on the journey I took with it. It's nonfiction.

I "told everybody what happened" in the most pedantic sense of the phrase. In a "too long; didn't read (tl;dr)" world, my story is quite simple: my friend and I met at a cafe after I hit a big career milestone, and he attempted to console me by telling me my job wasn't as hard as others in my profession. Also, there was chocolate.

Both my version and the tl;dr version are valid works of nonfiction. They convey the point. The difference is that one sets the scene in detail, outlining my psychological state, the warm intentions of my friend, and the myth that I quickly squelched. The other is the pamphlet version of the scene--a brief vignette that highlights the most necessary details.

Neither way is right nor wrong. However, as a fledgling nonfiction writer, you will need to decide how you're going to write your piece. Are you going to maintain that brevity is the soul of wit, or are you the type to paint a detailed picture with your words? You may also be somewhere in between—carefully choosing to elaborate here while trimming back the detail there to advance the discussion.

Those who have read my earlier books on the topic of writing- *How to Write a Book: A Book for Anyone Who Has Never Written a Book (But Wants To)* or *One Word at a Time: How to Write a Fiction Book for Beginners*- will appreciate that my definition of "how to" is a little different than others–another reflection of a decision you will have to make if you choose this path. I'm not able to hold your hand as you type to make sure that you put the perfect word in the perfect place every time. If I had that skill, this book would cost a great deal more. Instead, I'm going to coax you through the challenges, pump you up for progress, and agonize with you when it seems like nothing is calling you to be written. I will be honest and candid about the process and suggest strategies to help you get through the difficult parts.

We won't be going through topics like fact-checking, choosing the best adverb, or nonfiction-style theories. Instead, we'll look at the major types of nonfiction, including:

- Biographies, Autobiographies, Memoirs

- History and Travel

- Self-Help and How-To

- Philosophy, and Insight/Analysis

We'll look at what each of these types of work entails, as well as the various decisions writers may encounter when working on one of these pieces. The decisions you make as you write are always your own, and I encourage you to write exactly what you need to write. You can always go back and edit your work. Today's computing technology even allows us to save version histories so we don't lose any of our changes along the way. You can change your mind any time you want, so write from the heart and worry about it all working out later!

That being said, you can pull the final product together better if you are prepared for the questions and challenges you'll face along the way. A successful nonfiction piece is one that fulfills the dream of the author. It makes the right points, shares distinct information, asks the reader to consider the topic in greater detail, and can even challenge the reader's view of reality. Nonfiction work can be powerful, which is why I recommend that if you intend to write your own nonfiction piece, you aim to write a good one, whatever your personal definition of "good" may be. I do have a few ideas I would like to share with you on that topic.

In order to outfit you with the right tools for your writing journey, we'll take a look at some of the ways you can set yourself up for feeling good about your first nonfiction effort, from putting together your outline and choosing your style to gain helpful hints based on the various nonfiction genres.

I encourage all writers to read all chapters. You may be dead set on becoming a biographer, and I wish you all the best in that endeavor. But there's a chance that some of the thoughts I share in the "how-to" chapter may help you make decisions about your own piece. My own writing mentor encouraged me to not only read things that I wanted to read but to also read things I'd never considered. By doing so, I would be able to appreciate a greater range of styles, voices, tones, and approaches to different topics. He was absolutely correct—nearly every piece I write is partially inspired by something I've only just discovered in the process of writing that very book. From a turn of phrase to the pacing of the words, each book I write is a collection of everything I've learned since the previous effort.

My goal is to help you feel as confident in yourself as you can as a person who is starting to write a piece of nonfiction. As I've noted in my previous books, writing is a highly emotional, cerebral, and physical process. While I can't make the process any easier, I can be your writing buddy who can give you a tour through every step. I'll give you all the spoilers and do everything I can to ease your anxiety about the process.

Whether or not you write the next best seller after reading this book depends on a lot of factors. But I hope you feel inspired to start working on the outline for your nonfiction piece. And then, I hope you decide to keep going and research your topic and then start fleshing out the chapters. Write it. Stop worrying about it, and write it. But first, let's get acquainted with the task at hand.

WHAT MAKES "GOOD" NONFICTION?

I am oddly sensitive about the word "good." I know this isn't a book about what I, personally, like and don't like, but the word "good" is bandied about frequently in everyday conversation.

When referring to their first book, most first-time authors express the hope that it's "good," or "decent," or that it "doesn't suck." These are excellent aspirations in theory, but they don't really mean anything in the grand scheme of things.

Terms like "good" or "decent" and a book's suckitude—or lack thereof—are all vague and subjective. What is "good?" The opposite of "bad?" Okay, so what's "bad?" And then we tumble into a weird psycho-philosophical debate about conditional measurement and lived experiences. It gets messy fast.

When folks say they want to write a book that is good/decent/doesn't suck, they generally mean that they want to write a book that people want to read. People generally want to read books that they enjoy reading, page by page. That is, they want to enjoy the entire process, not slug through a few thousand words until they get to the good stuff.

This means that things like pace, tone, and style matter. The words you use are important. The way words flow, the conventions that you describe or omit, your grasp of grammar, and your ability to tell a story are still very important, even if the story you're telling is 100% factual.

"Pace" refers not only to the timeline of your book but to how quickly or slowly the average reader will be able to digest the content. Let's say, for example, you're writing a biography and wish to cover events from your subject's entire lifetime. You're going to have to consider how much time to devote to each section of your subject's life and which events to delve deeper into while skimming over others.

The tone of your book may be somewhat consistent, or it may shift depending on the topic at hand. You may approach certain topics with levity while providing very serious or shocking revelations about others. The words you choose help to set the tone. Consider, if you will, the difference between Snoopy's favorite "dark and stormy night" and "the sun, cracked in two by the horizon like an egg, spilling out light," as experienced by Margaret Atwood. These phrases represent not just opposite times of day, but two very different tones. It is the writers' artful manipulation of the words that set these unique tones.

"Style" is somewhat of an umbrella term for the process through which you choose the words you choose, put them in a particular order, shuffle them around until you find the version you like best, and keep going until you've run out of things to say. That may seem like a bit of a simultaneously direct and evasive answer, but style is very unique to every creator. The way you decorate your bedroom, the way you dress, how you take your coffee, and how you write are all part of your very own independent style. Your style may be heavily influenced by other individuals, but ultimately, what appears on the screen or paper in front of you is entirely your own.

There are ways to develop your pace, tone, and style, which I've discussed in my other books. If you've had a chance to read those, some of this information may seem familiar. The best way to develop anything, however, is to practice! Write away! Don't worry whether it's "good" or even "good enough." Instead, write because you want to practice. Visual artists have sketchbooks, so it stands to reason that those of us who work with words need practice as well. Get yourself a lovely notebook and supportive seat cushion, and write as much and as frequently as you feel called to write. Before you know it, you'll start feeling increasingly comfortable.

For those of us writing nonfiction pieces, pace, tone, and style are incredibly important. We use these devices to keep our readers reading. However, these aren't the only things to keep in mind when getting ready to write your nonfiction debut.

Let's take a deeper look into some of the most crucial factors to consider when planning your new literary venture.

A Shiny Topic

All of us aspire to be the kind of author who can write a book so beautifully that the audience won't care that it's incredibly boring. We want to believe we can take any mundane topic and polish it into incandescence with our carefully honed writing skills.

At the end of the day, however, we need to recognize the reality that current SEO recommendations include paragraphs that are at most three lines of text or two sentences. We've trained our brains to look for keywords, and our shrunken attention span is being pulled in multiple directions simultaneously. Perhaps you can write an absolutely stunning book about paint drying, but if you want to sell it, you've got to be a marketing genius. (You've also got to email me if you try this because I would love to hear your plans.)

Your choice of topic matters for so many reasons. If you choose an incredibly broad topic, you'll find yourself writing in overlapping circles trying to explain everything, creating a labyrinth of thought that will leave your audience trying to piece the details back together. Additionally, a broad topic requires a long time to explain. If you are working on a shorter essay, you may find that cramming a lot of details into a small space means you have to leave some information behind. Similarly, selecting a very specific topic for a longer article or book may force you to repeat yourself and stuff a bunch of unnecessary fluff into your writing just to meet the word count.

Furthermore, what is your angle on the topic? What particular details are you going to focus on in your nonfiction book? If you're writing a biographical piece on a political figure, for example, what aspects of their life are you going to highlight? What details of their political stance will you examine, and by what light? Are you writing from the standpoint of someone who agrees with this figure, or are you critiquing their actions?

Long ago, I took a writing class in which we pulled topics out of a plastic Jack-O-Lantern each month. We would then take our shiny new topics to the library and start to research. The goal was to write a different style of research piece involving that topic, but the topics themselves were astonishingly broad.

I once chose a slip of paper upon which the word "Madonna" had been typed. That's it. I had to choose whether I was going to write about Madonna, Mother of Christ, or Madonna, Queen of Pop. Then, I had to decide where I was going to go from there—there's no shortage of material on either of these remarkable women. I narrowed it down to comparing various historical artistic depictions of the Virgin Mary or detailing Madonna Ciccone's relationship with her mother—who passed away when Madonna was five years old—in the face of her own pregnancy announcement (long ago, remember). I chose the latter because the assignment had a ten-page limit, and I couldn't trust myself not to pick too many art samples.

The topic you select will appeal to a wide range of readers. The focus you choose will reduce the number of interested parties, but those who read it will likely be extremely interested and engaged. The angle you take will determine whether they write you nasty emails later.

Whether you're writing a biography, a history, a travel piece, or a how-to book, there will be some who agree with your observations and some who strongly do not. They won't necessarily write you nasty emails later—that was a bit of hyperbole, since the distribution of your book may be as minimal or global as you wish. However, if your goal is to write a "good" book, you'll need to prepare for some people to not find it that "good," after all.

You might think that writing nonfiction should be pretty neutral territory since you aren't making anything up—these are real people and things that you're writing about, after all! But even your most respectful, thoughtful, fact-driven writing will be bound to evoke some feelings. Many times, these feelings have nothing to do with your actual writing, but the realizations and thoughts that the reader had while they were digesting your piece.

Sometimes we write incendiary pieces on purpose. Persuasive pieces are fun, as are shocking exposes. If you've ever written a negative review for a business, you know the thrill of honestly emoting in the form of critique. Writing is art, and our emotions nearly always come peeking out in our craft. The angle you take when approaching your subject already speaks volumes about your thought process, so do you want to go for it and expose your true feelings, or play it neutral to appeal to a wider audience?

Consider who you want to read this book. Who are you speaking to? Who do you want to understand your message? Who do you think is going to read this book and take away all of the fine points and details you have written? Who is going to emotionally and mentally connect with your writing?

You may find that the angle from which you're approaching your topic and your audience don't really match well. The ten-page essay about Madonna and maternal relations would have been very different depending on who I wrote it for—I ended up choosing a high school audience because many of the interviews I found in my research discussed the pop singer feeling awkward in high school due to not having a mother figure in her life. I wanted to use this approach to connect with the insecurity we all feel during our teenage years, which can be amplified by any sense of being "strange."

Sometimes, writing feels like a puzzle. You've got lots of pieces sitting before you, and you just need to make them all fit. I think of brainstorming a topic more like looking through a kaleidoscope. You can clearly see what you're focused on at the end, but the light and mirrors play tricks on you, and the picture shifts any time you shift positions. As you're choosing your topic, I recommend rotating the lens a bit so you can view it from different angles. Focus on all sorts of different details, then spin the kaleidoscope to see the myriad of ways you can present your specific topic to your specific audience to get the desired effect.

Start conservative—what are some of the obvious topics you could choose? What is the first thing that comes to mind when you think about a specific issue, time period, or event? Some things are inextricably linked for better or worse, such as the Titanic and icebergs or Theodore Roosevelt and the National Park Service. But, of course, there's more to each of those topics than their existence or relationship to each other.

There are many ways to brainstorm your topic. Some writers use something like a Venn diagram, in which they start linking together interests and shifting angles to see how they lead back into each other. Others start with lists, with sub-topics branching off of each other, somewhat like a sports championship bracket. Still, others take advantage of the many technological advances that allow us to stay organized and write without losing track of all of our best ideas, such as writing apps, spreadsheets, and voice recorders. In one remarkable case, I knew a writer who would videotape herself talking through her topic.

If you're not sure where to start with all of these potential techniques, I recommend going back to the roots of writing with the analog paper-and-pencil technique. Find a blank piece of paper and a writing utensil of your choice, and jot down the first thing you think of when you think of writing a book. Abraham Lincoln. How to organize your closet. The way doing yoga daily saved your relationship. The history of Velcro.

Don't think too much about it. Don't worry about whether you should put the words in the middle of the page or at the top left or cattywampus across the entire right side. This isn't about doing things right. It's about doing them at all, and it's now that you are summoning the energy that is going to get you through this new book experience.

Now that you've got that idea down, write down everything that comes to mind after it. This "mind spew" can take the form of entire, cohesive sentences, clips and phrases, single words, or even drawings This is going to be harder than you expect because the judgmental pieces of your brain are going to try to talk you out of everything:

- *"You don't think anyone has examined Abraham Lincoln's mental health?"*

- *"Do you honestly believe there are 30,000 words about how flip flops changed the world?"*

- *"You are the only person who would read this."*

- *"You are not qualified to write about this topic."*

This very same voice has silenced some of the greatest authors who have never been published. Ignore it.

In fact, if you have a particularly poignant thought on your topic, go ahead and open a new document on your computer. Call it whatever you want. "New Book" is just fine. I've titled the first draft of this book "Nonfiction MS" because I haven't chosen the final title, and that's likely where you are now. Remove all thoughts of the finished book for now, and start typing out the words that need to be released. As I type this paragraph, I have no idea what the cover of this book will look like or even what it will look like after it goes through a few rounds of editing. There are pages of content you will never read because that's the reality of writing. Your document will live and breathe until it's published, and then it will continue to live and breathe in the minds and hearts of its readers.

When the book starts calling, answer. Start typing. Start listing. Start drawing. Keep the conversation going with yourself, but don't pick at yourself if you run out of ideas. That just means you need to approach it from another angle.

Sometimes I don't really know how finely tuned my topic is going to be until I've started outlining the table of contents. There have even been times when I was actively drafting the introduction and then realized that I needed to adjust a few things in order to make a coherent book appear.

At the same time, it's easy to think too much. If you try to apply too much logic to the art of choosing a topic, you will talk yourself out of the task. Whether I'm writing for myself or a client, my choice of topic, book organization, and research patterns depend on so many different factors—keywords, what's trending, and what I really want to write about. And ultimately, every time I sit down to write a book, it starts with a messy sheet of paper where I build the foundation by excavating the perfect topic.

So what is the "perfect topic?" In my opinion, it's the sweet spot where your passion and your interests collide with an inexplicable need to share this information with the entire world. In many cases, it's entirely illogical, which is why it's so easy to talk yourself out of doing it in the first place.

Writing a nonfiction book of any kind is going to take patience, time, energy, research, and careful planning. If you aren't all that invested in the topic, this will be agonizing. If you're mild to moderately interested in the topic, you might find yourself growing fond of and more fascinated by the topic as you uncover new details each time you dive into research. If you're moderately to severely obsessed with the topic, you'll find yourself trying to hold back before you go into encyclopedia mode. It's not that I don't encourage you to do so—I've just never written an encyclopedia, so I have no special advice for you!

But if you're planning on writing a biography, autobiography, memoir, history, travel, self-help, how-to, philosophy, or insight/analysis book, I've got you covered. Choose a topic that will stick. Start broad with a topic you could discuss in your sleep. Narrow it down. Cogitate on it. Ask yourself questions. Jot down your thoughts. Give it a few days, but not too many. Try typing a few paragraphs about it to try it on for size. If you don't find yourself getting sick of smartphone news alerts bringing up your topic every waking moment while you do this, you might just be onto something very good.

Fresh Perspective

The concept of perspective goes hand-in-hand with your topic. Essentially, the perspective is the angle from which you view your topic, and through which you interpret all data and research to support your topic. Ideally, every writer will have a different perspective, which when combined with their unique voice and particular style allows us to have many books that cover the same topic without them being word-for-word identical to each other.

There are very few topics that haven't been covered in some manner, which is why I urge you to ignore the voice of logic while you're hashing out your topic. I am completely aware that this is not the one and only "how to write nonfiction" book in the world. There are plenty of resources out there that cover all of the things I'll discuss in the following pages. If you have been researching this topic for a while, then you likely will not be surprised by the content of this book.

That being said, no one is going to write a book like I write a book. At least, I would prefer they didn't. My voice, tone, style, vocabulary, insistence on using "too," "very," and "so" so very too much, and examples are (hopefully) different from the experience you've had reading any other book on the matter.

Books inform and entertain, though each book offers a different ratio of each. For example, your seventh-grade history textbook was primarily written to inform, though the occasional witty quote and color photo/graphic/illustration would provide a momentary fresh breath of entertainment before digging into the next tragic historical scene.

Your book can be serious and strictly academic. Your book can be filled with comedic personal experiences and levity. In most cases, it will be a blend of both in what is or is about to become your signature style.

So, as you are contemplating your perspective on this topic, think of what makes sense. If you tend to have a witty take on things, it might be difficult for you to put a very serious spin on a major human rights issue, for example. That's not to say you can't, but just as certain actors play certain types of roles, authors tend to write books that share similarities in perspective. The process will likely be less stressful as well as more enjoyable for you—and your intended audience—if you do what comes naturally.

My perspective when writing these books is that of a friend or mentor. I write these books for writers who don't necessarily need more information on how to put sentences together, but who are eager for someone to hype them up during what is one of the most lengthy and agonizing processes of a new writer's life: the first book.

As I am not the only author with this perspective, I need to follow through to make sure this book is distinctive. My goal is to figure out why someone would want to read this book over every other friendly nonfiction writing book. A lot of what makes a book successful is marketing, but at the end of the day, world-class marketing can't save a book that isn't worth reading.

But we're getting a little ahead of ourselves here. One of my more non-traditional perspectives is that I don't necessarily think you need to be published in order to enjoy writing a good book. I also believe we shouldn't be too tied to the concept of perfection as we write since that tends to dampen the enjoyment of the process. If you've read my previous books, you'll know that I'm a huge proponent of getting the book written first, then worrying about editing and revision.

That being said, you can't really edit from a new perspective. You can add and subtract facts. You can change your arguments a bit, as long as you have the supporting information you need. You can add all the adjectives and adverbs you know. But changing the perspective of a story mid-stream is going to undoubtedly generate some major rewrites.

Some people enjoy extra challenges. I do not. I like it best when things go well and come easily so I can enjoy doing them. Therefore, I encourage those who are trying their hand at nonfiction for the first time to check their perspective before they get started to make sure it fits and feels comfortable. Take a look at this quick exercise to help you figure out where you're going, and whether it's right for you.

Exercise: Check Your Perspective!

As a writer, one of the most common questions I'm asked is, "How do you decide what to write about?" Essentially, they're asking me how I choose my topic and refine my perspective. Since it can be a multi-layered process, I thought we'd try walking through the general concept together to see how it can work.

Sometimes, yes, the entire framework of a book floats down from the Muses, and it is beautiful. Other times, however, I need to do a little critical finagling with the Muses, my mind, and my readers. Let's try out a few of the methods I use when I'm working on a new book.

Supplies needed:
- *paper/writing utensil and/or open, blank .doc file, set to your preferences*

- *a solid chunk of quiet, uninterrupted time (I recommend an hour, but most of us don't have that kind of luxury regularly)*

- *Device to do online research, or your local library*

Step 1: What do you want to write about? Identify it in the least possible number of words.

Dolly Parton. How to Write a Billboard Hot 100 Hit. Your personal health journey. How wearing only leggings changed your life. Wakatomika, Ohio. Be as broad and non-specific as you can here.

Step 2: Why? What about it?

Here you start to refine your interest. Let me use the current book you are reading as an example yet again.

For Step 1, I came up with "How to Write Nonfiction." I've already done "how to write a book," and "how to write fiction," and I've gotten some feedback from nonfiction author hopefuls that they'd love more resources.

For Step 2, here are the notes that I jotted down (transcribed from a small notebook my friend gifted me that says "Tacos and Naps" on the cover—not everything has to be "official writer-grade"):
- They asked you to

  ○ Don't always do what they asked you to

  ○ Unless it's a good idea

WHAT DO YOU WANT EVERYONE TO KNOW ABOUT NON-FICTION???????
- Everyone says it's easy

- It's not easy—it's easy to write crap, but good non-fiction takes effort

- Many people don't know what that effort entails

- Good topic

  - Needs to be interesting. Tell us why we care. Why should we read? Not too big, not too *(sic)* small. Look at things your way.

- Put it together right

- Make it sound good

- How do I help people understand how to put a book together?

- There are so many non-fiction styles. Do I know them all?

  - History

  - How-to

  - Biography

  - Self-help

    - Research all of these so you don't sound lost- you know this stuff.

Holistic or broad?

— All n/f readers? Focus on style? Focus on writing a good book?

As you can see, my original inspiration for writing this book was the knowledge that there were at least a handful of people who thought it would be a good idea. As my notes clearly indicate, I realized very early this wasn't a good enough reason to commit myself to the entire task.

So, I made myself pivot into my frustration at misconceptions about writing nonfiction. But then I started thinking about why I was frustrated, and I continued following myself down that rabbit hole.

Notice that I'm not doing any research here, but I'm making note of things I want to research. I actually have the word "research" highlighted in my original notes because I wanted to make sure I came back to that. You don't actually have to know everything there is to know about a topic before you decide to write a book about it. You just need enough interest and passion and an open mind to do the research to make it happen. When I started this book, I couldn't rattle off all of the different types of nonfiction. Obviously, I was familiar with them, but at that stage of the process, I wasn't a fine connoisseur of nonfiction.

I wasn't even entirely sure about the difference between an autobiography and a memoir (don't fret, we'll talk about it).

At this stage, you may feel incredibly discouraged about your topic, depending on what you used to define "why" you want to write this book. There may not be a lot of notes there. There doesn't need to be a lot of notes there. Not yet. Don't despair—dig deeper. Tenacity is the key.

Step 3: Time to Research!

Let me preface this by saying you're not about to research the whole book at once. That would be madness. However, at this point, you may accidentally stumble upon some fantastic resources for future use So, whether you do this on an electronic device or wander through the shelves at your local library, find some way of saving your search history.

We're about to embark on a journey to help us see how this topic currently exists in the literary world. You can call it "sizing up the competition" "finding your niche" "market research" or whatever feels most appropriate to your personal approach to the matter. I like to say I'm "finding my place on the shelves," even though I know most folks read my books digitally.

Do a search for your topic as identified in Step 1 —Google or card catalog—and look at what comes up. In most cases, it's going to be thousands upon thousands of relevant selections. If you're writing an autobiography, memoir, or philosophical book, you may turn up very few hits. This is both a blessing and a curse because you have free rein to write everything you know... but you still have to do it just one book at a time.

Look back at your notes from Step 2. Search again for your topic, only narrow it down by adding terms that you clearly feel passionate about. I used terms like "nonfiction for new writers" and "what makes good nonfiction," for example.

I mention doing this search in a public library because "going analog" actually has the advantage here. If you want to know what has been written about pre-colonization agriculture in what is today known as New England, you can search a few different terms in the library's search system—formerly known as a "card catalog"—jot down a few different suggested options, then physically search the aisles and look at, pick up, and even read a bit from all of the recommended resources. The advantage of doing the same thing online is that you can actually see all of the books on similar topics right there in front of you without relying on an algorithm. You don't have to scroll. You can just move side to side and up and down and get a feel for the size, quality, and depth of different resources without clicking a bunch of different things.

However, I fully acknowledge that the method does not work for all writers or all topics. When writing this book, I was somewhat lost for search terms, so I felt like getting lost at the library would leave me feeling more anxious than inspired!

If you're doing this step online instead of or in addition to wandering the bookshelves, you may also want to check out some of the free SEO tools offered online for inspiration. "SEO" stands for "Search Engine Optimization," and many marketing professionals use these tools to help them understand what terms people are searching for and how often they're conducting these searches. These terms are known as keywords.

While this step will become important again if you decide to market your book for sale, right now you're just looking for keywords related to your ideas. I personally don't like to look too heavily at the keyword ranking—this is an indicator of how popular a search term is—unless I actually need a certain number of clicks, purchases, or downloads in order to be successful.

Instead, think of this as listening in to all of your potential readers telling you what really interests them. Find inspiration in the curiosity of others, and make it your goal to answer those questions and satiate those minds... whoever' they may be.

Step 4: Finding Your Readers

Speaking of your readers, another big influence in how you refine your perspective is figuring out who you're writing for... meaning, who is your audience?

This could be very broad- "young adult" or very specific- "young adults in the Midwest with an interest in livestock farming but not necessarily 4H." If you're trying to market your book for sale or shop for a publisher, you may want to be precise about your audience. If you just want to write for the sake of watching words appear on the page—which I do admit is very satisfying—then you might think about which of your friends and family members you would allow to read your book, if any. Your reader can be absolutely no one, in which case, you can skip this step entirely.

But, if you're interested in exploring this topic, there are a few different ways to narrow things down. If you've done an online SEO search, you may have discovered that keyword tools often have analytical functions that allow you to look at the demographics of who is searching for what. If you haven't gone online yet and you'd like to discover these fun tools, fear not—I've linked a few options in the Resources chapter.

Consider demographic research an insight into the readers' trains of thought. It's ok to compare it to your train of thought from Step 2, but don't start worrying about whether your idea is good enough or if you should change it to appeal to the masses. Instead, consider this a look at how others are approaching the topic to see how you may be able to refine your perspective. You don't have to take this information to heart but as more of a suggestion. You also don't have to drill down to the level of "What type of toothpaste do my readers use?" but rather, get a general idea of who shares your passion and interest in this topic. What's their education level? What other books do they read? What kind of music do they listen to? What's their level of social interaction like?

You may be wondering why all of this matters, and to some extent, it doesn't. I believe you should write whatever book your heart desires. That being said, if you want people to read and enjoy your book, you're going to have to write your book in a way that they will *want* to read it and *easily* enjoy it. You will need to use words and concepts that they can understand. You will need to make references that are familiar to them. You want to write a book that doesn't leave your audience asking for a refund.

By knowing who your reader is, you can avoid overwhelming, angering, and confusing the people who choose to read your book. A kindergartener and a poet laureate are going to have very different vocabulary and reading comprehension skills, so choose who you're writing for and stick with it.

Step 5: Put It Together

Sometimes, I start this process and everything becomes crystal clear right away. I end up doing the research steps mostly to solidify my perspective and make sure I'm on the right path.

Sometimes, I do all the steps and I still have no clue what I'm doing. There are a few ways out of this:

1. **More research**- Rather than trying too hard to make things fit, intensify your research. I like to copy the link to each of my resources along with any interesting information found at that resource in a Google doc. Eventually, something will spark my interest, and hey! Didn't I see something about that back on that one site, a few clicks ago? It's really the definition of digging a deeper hole, but the likelihood of finding literary gold is pretty high. As you keep going, ideas, theories, questions, and opportunities will start to form in your mind. Nearly every time I've gone digging, I've found exactly what I was looking for—maybe it took a few days or weeks, but it was there.

2. **Adjust the topic**- There are no impossible topics. But maybe there really isn't very much interest *or* material out there to write about "Opossum UFO Encounters." But what about "Nocturnal Animals and Paranormal Experiences?" Maybe your

topic really is too narrow or too broad, and rotating the kaleidoscope through which you view your topic ever so slightly will refocus your topic to meet your level of investment in writing this book.

3. **Adjust the audience**- If you're having a hard time figuring out how to write about your topic to certain folks, consider whether you're writing to the wrong crowd. There is an audience for everything, I assure you. Find your people. This may mean searching for social media or online communities that share your passion for your topic. I've actually done this a few times, and I met some very cool friends along the way!

4. **Delete, delete, delete**- I don't recommend this. You will regret this if only because you'll try to remember the references you looked at, and you'll never find them again because you deleted all of your notes. Keep the notes and become a valuable asset at Trivia Night.

As with any of my suggestions, I recommend you look at these steps and take away from it what you need. You don't have to do everything I say exactly. There is no "punishment" if you don't "do it right." In our world, that phrase is spelled "do it write," because as long as you are creating and feeling motivated and generally positive about the experience, you're on the right track. If at any time you read one of my exercises or suggestions and say "That's not how I'd do it," then I encourage you to do it exactly as you see fit. I'm a mentor, not a drill sergeant!

Be patient with yourself. I'm sure some writers are able to generate an idea while making their morning coffee and have the whole thing outlined by chapter by the time they finish breakfast. I'm not one of those people. I can't tell you how many times I've looked at the screen and thought "That will never work." I've even been right a few hundred times!

At the end of the day, there will be people who simply don't "get" your book. They'll find your sense of humor insufferable, and your style annoying, and they'll be more or less turned off by everything you've done to write your book. That's fine because you're not writing your book for that person.

Always write for yourself, but if you are interested in publishing, selling, or somehow sharing your book with others, consider carefully the ideas that came to mind and the things you discovered through this exercise!

Thoughtful Organization

Now that you have your topic and you know how you're going to explore it, it's time to consider how you're going to organize the book. While writing a stream-of-consciousness mind blurt of everything you are thinking can be very satisfying and a great way to get over a writer's block hump, it's not ideal for many nonfiction readers.

Furthermore, even if you are writing just for yourself and like the idea of a good stream-of-consciousness mind blurting, thoughtful organization can make your life a lot easier. No matter the genre you pick, the topic you select, or the perspective through which you gaze, putting energy into organizing your book is never a bad idea.

First, a book is long. Even if you've got all of your ideas airtight and ready to go, you'll still likely need to stand up and stretch, go to the restroom, have a snack, and occasionally sleep while you're writing it. For most writers, 1,000-3,500 words is a pretty good day's writing session, but as I've said in my other books, don't hold yourself to this type of standard or you'll be miserable. How long it takes to write 1,000-3,500 words depends on how focused you are, how many interruptions you have, how many times you get lost in thought, how many times you have to look up synonyms and quotes, and so on. I have spent 8 hours on an assignment and walked away with 500 usable words for my efforts simply due to the amount of research I needed and my ability to concentrate.

What I'm trying to say is that a lot can happen in 1,000 words. You may not remember what has happened in the past 1,000 words. You may sit down tomorrow and not necessarily recall what you wrote two days ago. When you're writing, focused on a point, and trying to create a very big picture using very small-seeming words, you can become overwhelmed and forgetful.

Organization can keep you going in these difficult times. If you can refer to your notes and know exactly what you've already covered, you can skip the part where you repeat yourself *ad nauseam* and save yourself a lot of time and frustration.

Personally, I like to start with an outline. I know I'm going to have an Intro and a Conclusion, and that a Resources chapter is highly likely, so I start off with those. Then I look at the key areas I want to cover. For my goal of explaining the different types of nonfiction and how to explore them, I needed to figure out how to include them all. So, I grouped them:

1. Intro

2. ???

3. Biographies, Autobiographies, and Memoirs

4. History and Travel

5. Self-Help and How-To

6. Philosophy and Insight/Analysis

7. Conclusion

8. Resources

9. Intro

10. ???

11. Biographies, Autobiographies, and Memoirs

12. History and Travel

13. Self-Help and How-To

14. Philosophy and Insight/Analysis

15. Conclusion

16. Resources

So how did I figure out how to group them? That was probably the toughest part. Chapter 3 was perhaps the most obvious since those three genres are closely related. The rest required significant research.

I spent weeks looking into some of the top challenges experienced and discoveries made by professional writers while writing these topics. I dug into some of the uniting factors that can directly help guide writers who choose these genres, and grouped them by what we'll call "really important things to know." The challenges faced by self-help and how-to writers are often the same, so I put them together, for example. This will, of course, make more sense when you've read the chapters, but since we're using this book as an example of the process, bear with me for now.

Next, I started to make notes on what I wanted each chapter to contain:

6. Philosophy and Insight/Analysis

    1. Avoiding a stream-of-consciousness disaster

a. HOW:

    i. Focus

    ii. Clarity

    iii. knowing the point you're trying to prove

2. Make people care without holding them hostage or becoming a bully

These are the earliest, little, baby stages of chapters. Feel free to go back to the table of contents or flash forward to the chapter itself to see how this went, but suffice it to say, things have changed.

As I dove further and further into my research, I started making more and more connections between my initial impressions of how things would go and the reality of the facts. In this case, it was more of a fine-tuning exercise than a full rewrite, but I can assure you that you'll usually find yourself making notes in your outline, then using the cut/paste/rearrange method of putting related sources and points together until you've finally shuffled all the puzzle pieces into a working roadmap of your literary journey.

I am aware that there are many people out there who aren't big fans of outlines. I appreciate that, and I've mentioned a few alternative methods to outlining in my other books. What I want you to take away from this is that you have the ability to re-do and refine your book's organization as much as you need to until it feels "right."

I know some folks really enjoy the book template apps and software available to help them get organized. I haven't actually tried any myself because I am old, cranky, and set in my ways, but I firmly believe that the best way for you to visualize your book is whatever system you develop. I know folks who use Magic Markers and multi-colored pieces of construction paper. Some writers just write everything down as it comes, potentially working on several different chapters each day. Then they reconstruct everything during editing and add whatever is needed to make these ideas flow.

If you have no idea where to start, try my outline idea. If you end up staring at a blank screen and a blinking cursor for more than 15 minutes, give up. Try writing an outline in a notebook. Do a vision board. Meditate about what it would take for you to visualize the order you want to work in. As long as you continue to feel inspired, excited, and not too terribly stressed, there is no wrong answer here.

Author's Note: Being Obvious

When it comes to writing some types of nonfiction, such as histories, biographies, and even some travel pieces, it's tempting to write things in chronological order. In fact, that's probably the easiest way for an author to organize many of these topics. It makes sense. Life happens chronologically, so you don't have to move things around in order to share your perspective with your audience.

If you feel this is the best way to present your ideas on your topic, then please proceed. But if you're trying to explain the "why" and "how" of something, you might need to draw on facts from around the world and across the expanse of history.

Let me simplify with an example. Let's say you're writing a book about how the development of dependable electricity in the United States has impacted the economy. One way to write this book would be to start with the dawn of the modern economy and how things were before the advent of electricity. Then you might look at the invention of electricity and the different areas that have benefited from it, such as manufacturing, communication, and agriculture. You might compare the influx of dependable electricity across the country with economic development over time, following the National Grid rollout.

OR! You could arrange the book by the different areas you wish to examine. One chapter can review pre-electricity manufacturing practices, what changed in the early 1900s when electricity came along, how practices have developed since then in direct relation to electricity becoming common, and the overall economic impact of those changes for mass production, market value, and so forth. The next chapter could be communication, starting with options prior to electricity, the changes, or how keeping in contact with others has now become an imperative part of social function and employment, and so on and so forth until you've examined all of the parts of the economy you wish to discuss.

As you can see, these are two very different books that include the same information. But as the writer, you get to choose how you present your facts. When doing so, please consider:

- *What do you want to read?*

- *What do you want to write?*

- *What do you think will really help each point you make stand out?*

- *Which will feel the most organic?*

Most readers don't read an entire book in one sitting, as much as they probably want to. As a result, readers generally don't like books that skip around too much. "In 1912, our hero went to Washington DC to discuss human rights, just as he had done in 1842, but this time was a little different." I strongly encourage you to consider how easy it is going to be for your reader to keep up with you when organizing your book, even if that means stepping away from the more obvious organization method and moving things around to make them more digestible.

Ultimately, staying organized as a writer will help your audience stay organized as a reader. Have you ever watched a movie in the theater, stepped out to use the restroom, returned, and had a brief moment of disorientation in which you thought you were in the wrong theater? The characters and scene changed so quickly that your brief absence left you completely disoriented. This can happen to readers, too. Present information in a way that builds their knowledge, rather than throwing facts at them.

As writers, our relationship with our readers is complicated. On one hand, we have the ability to write any book we want about any topic, including all of our opinions, and put it together as well as the thoughts in our heads. On the other hand, if we want people to read our writing, we need to create something palatable for other people.

You get to choose who that audience is, and how many people you're willing to include in it. You are not limited in saying what you want about whatever you want, but there are consequences. If you head into defamation territory or start telling flat-out lies, then there's a possibility someone might sue you for libel.

Your readers also have the right to not like your book. Some of them won't understand it. I once signed up for a course during my undergrad days, only to open up the textbook and realize it made no sense to me. I dropped the class immediately. No one wants to suffer.

Only you can make the reading experience enjoyable and informative for your audience. If you spend some time selecting your topic, take care when whirling through the kaleidoscope of potential perspectives, and present your ideas in a meaningful, provoking, direct manner, you have a higher chance of making that happen.

Now, let's take a look at the various genres or styles that fit under the nonfiction umbrella, along with some special considerations to keep in mind when attempting your first foray into each!

BIOGRAPHIES, AUTOBIOGRAPHIES, AND MEMOIRS

E veryone has a story. Everyone has hopes, dreams, fears, opinions, theories, and ideas. Every life is a unique experience.

The stories of others can inspire us. Understanding how other individuals processed trauma and turmoil, discovered their talents, or made important decisions can give us insight into how these actions or reactions changed the entire world... or made a lasting impact on the individual experiencing them.

Biographies, autobiographies, and memoirs are nonfiction styles that share someone's life story. You may wish to write the entire life story of an individual, or in some cases, the history of a group of individuals, such as a band or a school of artists. You may wish to focus on your subject's specific contributions to history, art, science, technology, sports, or any other field. You may instead focus on their personal journey, or how their views developed over time based on events that occurred during their lifetime.

Your topic can be very well-known, or very personal. You could focus on how the Civil War impacted Abraham Lincoln's mental health, or you could explore how working the third shift has formed your sleeping and eating habits. You can write about yourself, someone you know, or someone you've never met. Whether they're in the here and now or the hereafter, any human experience can be the topic of a nonfiction book.

Biographies, autobiographies, and memoirs are our way of capturing the human experience, making sense of it, and sharing it with others. Though we may be writing about the life of another human being, we may never have the chance to actually interact with them. Therefore, the perspective of these books is purely our own.

As a result, it's often helpful to really nail down where you plan to go with these types of books before you get started, hence why I put them immediately following the chapter about planning and organizing your book! You can tell someone's life story in a series of short tales, like an elder relative may have shared stories with you, or go with a factual chronological account of events. Your goal is to share who that person is or was, and why and how their story can impact others. The choices you make surrounding the topic, perspective, and organization of the piece will undoubtedly influence the type of impact made, however.

One special consideration of biographies, autobiographies, and memoirs is the audience. Some of us lead rather. er, *sordid* lives, shall we say. That is to say, there are certain details about everyone's lives that we tend to avoid sharing with particular audiences. A book about Elvis written for a child in elementary school and for someone from the Boomer generation may have very different candid details, for example.

Furthermore, the amount of detail you might wish to include will vary between audiences. A more seasoned audience may be interested in the fine details of how and why Paul McCartney composed "And I Love Her," while in other instances, it may be more than enough to mention that this event happened at all.

All told, while every life is fascinating, not every detail is relevant. When writing biographies, autobiographies, and memoirs, it's a good idea to check yourself with how many important dates and events you wish to include compared to the points you're trying to make and the journey you're trying to share. If I were writing my own memoir, for example, I probably wouldn't include the fact that I had a Cabbage Patch doll drawn in icing on my third birthday cake, even though on that particular day, it meant the absolute world.

It is possible—and in some cases even imperative—to focus on a single era, time, or event in a person's life. You may wish to take a good, hard look at your topic and perspective to make sure it's going to give you enough room to explore without forcing you to write thousands of pages to express your ideas—unless that's your overall goal. But for those of us who are looking to write a modestly-sized book about something we enjoy, fine-tuning these areas will help you avoid burnout and keep you from abandoning your project.

Organization is also important in these types of books because it is very easy to get dates and events confused. Once you've written so many sentences like, "In June 1822, he turned 18. Shortly afterward, on July 18, his 22-year-old brother...", you'll find that your brain starts spinning a little. Having a solid system of organization can help you stop the spinning by focusing on real and true facts in an order that makes sense. This will also help you effectively meander through an entire lifetime of material to focus on the events that best support your ideas.

We'll look at many different things to keep in mind throughout this chapter, but as we're establishing each type of nonfiction and how to write it, I wanted to take the time to touch back to the points that can help you create a nonfiction book that you'll actually enjoy writing.

Read on to learn more about things to keep in mind when writing biographies, autobiographies, and memoirs.

What's the Difference?

If you're like me, the differences between a biography, an autobiography, and a memoir are some vague concepts that you understand but have never really needed to dive into… until the moment you absolutely do.

As a writer, it's a good idea to keep yourself educated about writing, but no human being is expected to know the intimate nuances of every technical aspect of their career. That's why references and resources exist. In that spirit, let's take a look at biographies, autobiographies, and memoirs, each in more detail, so you can decide which option is best for your big book idea.

Biographies

Of the three, a biography is the most easily recognizable and definable. This is the story of a person or sometimes people, as told by you. The subject can be absolutely anyone—from a cultural icon to your next-door neighbor—as long as it isn't yourself.

There are many reasons why someone might choose to write a biography. They may wish to connect an individual's life experiences to their contributions to society. Perhaps the biography is intended to reveal that person's personality or outlook. A biography can focus on struggles, triumphs, or a bit of both.

It's also possible to write a biography about multiple people. Earlier, I gave examples of a musical band or a school of artists, but you can also write a biography about an entire community of people, like the settlers of Roanoke or the underground gambling market of New York City.

When writing about multiple people, you'll want to be careful about how much you focus on each individual. In some cases, such as writing about ancient civilizations, you won't have too many specific details about each and every individual. On the other hand, if you're writing about a famous music group, you might have more details than you know what to do with at first.

Most biographies include the following details:

- Name of a person or people (Frank Sinatra, The Anasazi culture, Corvette enthusiasts)

- Information about that person's birth, or establishment of a group of people (born in *place* on *the date*, fossils indicate roamed the area in *a year*, founded by *a person* in *a year*)

- Their personal life (upbringing, family life, and relationships)

- Their educational experiences (school, oral and written traditions, practical experience in a field)

- What they did (life events, achievements, and challenges)

- Why they are important in their field, to a group of people, or society as a whole

They can also include:

- Interviews and introspection

- Theories as to their motivation, inspiration, or purpose

- Media or scandals surrounding the subject

- Analysis of their overall impact in their field, on a group of people, or on society as a whole

You can approach a biography from many directions. You can paint your subject as a hero, as a villain, or neutrally. I mentioned earlier that you'll want to have a certain sense of passion for your project, but that can mean any type of enthusiasm or energy you have about discussing the topic. It is not unheard of for someone to write a biography that critiques or disparages the actions and decisions of the subject.

You can also choose to be as "safe" or illicit in your portrayal as you wish—as long as you remember your audience. When writing about Madonna, for example, I could have taken the route of exploring her more risqué performances and publications, but it wasn't the right audience. Instead, I tried to write the story people didn't expect—a heartwarming tale of a woman who grew up motherless and longed to become a mother. I felt my audience was less interested in rehashing the sensational news stories and more interested in understanding who Madonna is as a person.

As you start the process of choosing your biography topic and perspective, consider what story you're going to tell. Who are you sharing this story with, and what do you hope for them to learn from this? We'll get a little more into the research and writing process for biographers in the next chapter, but for now, I recommend taking your time when getting organized to make sure you've got a well-established plan before you get started.

Autobiographies

Autobiographies, on the other hand, tell the story of one very specific person: you.

An autobiography may be written in the first person or as a third-person narrative, but the main subject is always the author themself. Regardless of the style or perspective, an autobiography is always a self-portrait.

The content of an autobiography is generally the same as a biography, including your birth, early life, education, job experiences, as well as the pinnacles and pratfalls you have experienced to date.

At first glance, this seems like a super-easy task. After all, we have an innate expertise in our own insights and motivations. You don't actually need to do any research, right?

Well, kind of. See, you still need to have a perspective, and you might want to pare down your topic a bit to focus on a particular facet of your life. But writing an autobiography means having to reflect on the events of your life. You may need to look up dates. You may wish to interview people who were there for these specific times to get their angle on the situation. You might want to tie in current events, which means creating a timeline and getting a feel for what those events entailed, and why it's important for you to reflect upon them.

But most of all, you want to be organized. We'll talk a little bit more about what writing a book about yourself entails, but think of how frequently your thoughts go bouncing around when you open the "Halls of Memory". How do you decide how much context to include, and how many "scenes" to include? Again, we'll get to that bit in a part, but keep it in mind that most autobiographies are not merely a writer jotting down, "Here's what I thought today and what I think it means." That's more of a philosophical type of book, which we'll explore in a few chapters.

At the core of the organization is often the "why" of book writing. As we discussed several times in Chapter 1, writers of "good" nonfiction ask themselves why they're doing what they're doing many, many times. Sometimes it's more of a moaning curse, but we're looking at "why am I writing this book" from the standpoint of "what are my intentions for writing this book, who do I want to read it, and what do I hope they are going to gain from it."

There are many reasons to want to tell your story:

- Because of your contributions to society

- Because you overcame a struggle and wish to inspire others

- Because you happen to need a little money and you have some information to share

- Because your side of a very important story needs to be told

- Because your story is your legacy that you wish to share with future generations

- Because you simply feel like it

Any of these, or others, is a valid reason to start the writing process, but again, I urge you to take into consideration how much it means to you that other people read and enjoy this book. You don't have to have a reason to tell a tale, but you do have to make some kind of point while doing it, or else the readers will feel confused and betrayed, as discussed earlier.

Paying close attention to your autobiography's organization can ensure that you maintain a grip on your intended audience throughout your tale, as they'll be able to follow you easily along the trail you've blazed.

Memoirs

Some people use the terms "autobiography" and "memoir" interchangeably, and that's... sort of true. Much like the relationship between the rectangle and the square, a memoir is always an autobiographical piece, but not every autobiography can be considered a memoir.

Memoirs typically focus on a specific event, time period, or facet of a person's life, such as their struggle with mental health in high school, that one time when they launched a new app that sold millions, or their experiences with the loss of a loved one.

Like autobiographies, they're typically told in the first person—but not always. Also, like autobiographies, they can include information like your name, experiences growing up, education, and career stats. But unlike autobiographies, they focus mostly on a particular experience or set of events and include the actions, reactions, and emotions of that time period. It may include how things were before the catalyst of your book, as well as how things are now, but unlike an autobiography, a memoir is a rumination on a very specific topic or event within your life.

I mentioned earlier that a finely-tuned topic frequently has a more specific audience, and that notion is sustained in the spirit of the memoir. Whether the tone of your memoir is triumphant or traumatic, you'll need to decide who you want to read this book as you're putting together your notes. Are you writing for people who are now in your shoes, experiencing the same things you've survived, or are you writing for those who have someone in their lives who has faced these things? Are you providing education for people who aren't familiar with the challenges and triumphs you've been through? The way you frame your story and the level of personal detail you include may vary depending on who you want to read your book.

Ultimately, when you are writing a biography, autobiography, or memoir, you are taking on the responsibility of presenting an actual human being's life to your audience. The art of representation is monumental—especially if you're writing about yourself. Let's take a look at how you can use research and writing techniques to really let your audience know about your subject.

How to Talk about Someone You May Not Know

Personally, I get nervous about writing biographical pieces, especially if the person I'm writing about is still alive. That means there's a chance they'll read it. What if they aren't impressed, or worse yet, threaten to sue me?

Thankfully, that hasn't happened to date, and I believe it's because I take extreme care to write about these individuals. I write as though I am ghostwriting their autobiography, taking care to highlight the things they're passionate about and being fair and fact-based when discussing any controversy.

Of course, you may not be interested in painting your subject in a warm light. Critical pieces are just as important as praise, and sordid lives are often the most entertaining. These are the pieces that are more likely to ruffle some feathers.

When you're writing a biography, you *must* research to avoid legal entanglements. There are two specific reasons for this:

1. Libel is the publication of writing, pictures, cartoons, or any other medium that exposes a person to public hatred, shame, disgrace, or ridicule, or induces an ill opinion of a person, and is not true.

Actions for libel result mainly from news stories that allege crime, fraud, dishonesty, immoral or dishonorable conduct, or stories that defame the subject professionally, causing financial loss either personally or to a business (Associated Press Style and Libel Guide 251).

1. Defamation is a statement that injures a third party's reputation. The tort of defamation includes both libel (written statements) and slander (spoken statements). State common law and statutory law govern defamation actions, and each state varies in its standards for defamation and potential damages. Defamation is a tricky area of law as the lines between stating an opinion versus a fact can be vague, and defamation tests the limits of the First Amendment freedoms of speech and press (https://www.law.cornell.edu/wex/defamation).

The phrase "defamation is a tricky area of law" is enough to stop me in my tracks. I, personally, do not wish to be embroiled in any sort of legal case. I don't want to hire a lawyer. I don't want to be sworn in or cross-examined. I want to write books, have fun, and get paid.

Therefore, I make it a point to carefully vet all of my resources. Most of the time, it's pretty easy to do so with a single click. I know you're not supposed to judge a book or a webpage by its cover, but if I find myself on a site laden with Blingees, last updated in August 2006, it isn't a bad idea to doubt its veracity.

As writers, we also have the ultimate "get-out-of-jail-free card," which is citing our resources. Phrases like "According to (resource)," or "The story told about this event in (resource)," can be very helpful for exposing the fact that you did not invent this information, but are merely drawing conclusions based on what others have published. Of course, it's a good idea to cite your resources anyway because plagiarism is an actual sin. Quoting, on the other hand, is good for back-link SEO, not to mention the soul.

Bear in mind that there are many different types of resources, as well. Most of us tend to start looking up books and conducting Google searches, but those aren't the only possible sources. One fun element unique to biographies is the chance to conduct interviews, either with your subject or other experts on your subject, such as family members, historians, archaeologists, and experts in your subject's field. Look for published diaries or journals, television or audio recordings, and transcripts, too.

I'd like to take a deeper dive into what it means to vet your resources since this can be so crucial to aspiring biographers. It can mean the difference between a compelling, well-received book and a mistake-laden flop.

Author's Note: The Difference between Accurate and Anecdotal

Technology is a godsend for writers. We have all sorts of devices that can record everything we say or do, so we can play them back and accurately describe and transcribe the scene. However, technology hasn't always been around. Sometimes we have to rely on how other people have described and transcribed these scenes.

You've probably heard the phrase from Robert Evans: "There are three sides to every story: your side, my side, and the truth." Meaning, there's the perspective of Person 1, the perspective of Person 2, and the actual, factual account of the situation. To make things even more complicated, frequently everyone who is in any way impacted by, adjacent to, or knew someone who knew someone in connection to a notorious person will come out of the woodwork to share their thoughts. I'm not saying they are necessarily liars, but we frequently embellish or misremember things when we're excited or nervous, which most of us are when we're being interviewed.

Anything you read that is not a verbatim transcription of an interview, speech, or conversation will be considered anecdotal. Even a person recalling an experience may not remember exactly what they said, or the specific order of events, especially if it wasn't particularly important to them at that moment. Do you recall the exact words you said when you learned how to ride a bicycle for the first time? Or which sock you put on first on the day you met your partner or spouse? You may remember that you shouted, or that you were wearing socks with cats on them, but some of the details fall off with time and more important events.

Generally speaking, if this anecdotal information is considered valid—meaning it's been published or otherwise approved or licensed by the individual or their estate—then it's not very risky to use it.

The only way to be fully accurate is to use original recordings, diaries, letters, or notes from the party involved. This can get a little sketchy if you're working with subjects who are long deceased because the interpretation and translation of what they said, wrote, or painted on cave walls will be subject to the perspective of the interpreter.

Unfortunately, the only way to write a completely accurate account of a person's life is to interview them directly, which may or may not require the invention of time travel. What we can do, however, is treat anecdotes for what they are: the best possible retelling we have. Wording like, "In his 1980 interview, (subject's) childhood friend Bill stated that..." or "Newspaper accounts at the time stated that (subject)...." You can only tell the truth as it is reported to the masses.

Also on the table is the semi-fictional take on a person's life, known as "biographical fiction." While the events portrayed in the writing are true, perhaps we don't know exactly who was present, or exactly what words were spoken. For example, we're not entirely sure where everyone was sitting during the signing of the Declaration of Independence, but if you're writing about the scene, you may need to have Benjamin Franklin tap Thomas Jefferson on the shoulder to make a point. We don't necessarily know whether that actually happened, but it's reasonable to think that it could have. It's also not incendiary or potentially defamatory.

This style is common among historical and biographical works intended for younger readers, though it's certainly not limited to any particular age group.

Generally speaking, biographical fiction is shelved with other works of fiction, but given the intense overlap with nonfiction, I wanted to give it a call-out. Everything in this book can apply to writers of semi-fictional biographical or historical pieces as well.

When writing a biography, understanding the difference between accurate and anecdotal resources can help avoid trouble later, with your audience or your subject.

Regardless of whether you plan to paint a rosy portrait of your subject or share your overwhelming disapproval of them, it's important to most writers to talk about other people in a way that will not impact them legally. You don't have to be nice, of course—you just have to avoid making things up. Choosing your resources carefully and understanding the difference between accurate and anecdotal information can help you with that endeavor.

In a nutshell, when you're talking about other people, it's a good idea to make sure your vision for your book aligns with the resources you have. A highly clinical book is going to need more accurate resources, but by framing and presenting anecdotal information as just that, you can avoid legal and reputational calamity.

An Actual Anecdotal Biographical Piece for Your Consideration:

Perhaps the best advice I can give you is what I learned from a professor in college. Though the topic of the course wasn't specifically about publishing, we students would sometimes wheedle our professor into discussing and describing his trials and tribulations in being published. I'll preserve his anonymity simply because it's been decades since we've lost touch, but suffice it to say, he was a well-recognized author who had received many prestigious awards, and I was lucky to study under him.

When it came to biographies, his advice was to treat the subject with respect. Even if we hated our topic with unwavering passion, he recommended we give a biographical subject—alive or deceased—respect as a living being. It's best to use your words to describe why they are such a horrible person—don't attempt to invent anything or go with low-blow insults. If written well, a nonfiction piece can reveal exactly how the writer feels about a certain topic without resorting to name-calling or toeing the line of libel. Don't put words in your subject's mouth—let them do all the talking.

You may or may not disagree with this particular advice, but it's certainly something to keep in mind when you're writing about someone else. You don't have to say your worst enemy is the best guy you've ever met, but you also don't have to refer to him as "that stupid idiot" in every paragraph.

But what if you do know the person you're writing about? The chance to actually interview a person about their experiences is one of my favorite things about nonfiction because you can actually tune in to their telling and understand events and circumstances through their first-hand account. But it can also be a bit nerve-wracking to know that the person you're writing about will, in fact, be checking in on what you've said.

I strongly encourage you to record whatever interview sessions you have, whether that be an audio or video recording. Remember that you need to get permission before recording someone, but if the individual is aware and accepting of the fact that you're writing about them, that's generally not hard to do.

Personally, when I'm writing about someone with whom I've actually interacted, I like to try to capture the overall vibe of speaking with them. What is their body language like as they recount their tales? Do they have certain inflections in their voice or little mannerisms that are noteworthy?

Not only does painting the picture of your subject help invite the reader into the situation, but it can also actually make the writing process a little easier. For most of us, writing about a real, tangible scenario that we have actually encountered is a little more familiar and comfortable than writing about something completely foreign to our experiences. Visual artists have used models for portraits since the dawn of creation, so it's really no surprise that literary artists should do the same. Plus, it's really nice to be able to email or phone your subject to clear up any questions you might have.

Alas, writing a biography about a living person in your sphere of existence isn't always possible. That being said, it is entirely possible to use some of the techniques you would use when interviewing a subject while doing your research.

For example, you might have very specific questions for George Washington, and while it's impossible to communicate with him via traditional means, you can still ask those questions. Instead of posing them over the phone or in person, you'll have to answer them by conducting a lot of research. Forming specific questions that are pertinent to your topic and perspective and finding the answers for them can be a great way to refine your research and help you choose resources that will actually help you, rather than repeat all of the things you've already learned.

Writing a biography can be a complicated, anxiety-inducing experience, but you can gain control of the fear by gathering adequate, accurate resources and bringing a bit of basic respect to the table. When in doubt, stick to the facts, and let your words express your emotions. This is true of all types of writing, particularly when you're actively avoiding legal consequences.

Next, let's look at how to speak warmly and accurately about and not defame yourself... and yes, that is kind of a thing.

How to Talk About Yourself

At first glance, the idea of talking about yourself may seem pretty simple. After all, you were there, you have a generally good idea of what you said and what happened, so you should be able to describe events and conversations in detail, right?

There are two slight hiccups in this idealistic view of autobiographies and memoirs, however.

First, there's that thing about multiple perspectives and individual views. Everyone who has a memory of an event remembers it from their own perspective, as mentioned earlier. One interesting example of this phenomenon is the conversations that occur when you ask someone where they were on the date of a major event. Common examples include "when JFK was assassinated," or "on 9/11," not that the actual events have to be significantly tragic. If you survey your family about where they were when Aunt Helen dropped the birthday cake in the swimming pool, you'll get the same rousing round of different perspectives.

Then there's the traditional unreliability of memory itself. I'm not attempting to insult your IQ or your memory, but most of us lack 100% recall. With all due respect, most folks don't have the full picture, even if they were the subject of the portrait. It's not that we're lying to ourselves or anyone else, but that our brains are weird things that remember whatever they want to remember.

For example, we may remember the idea of what someone said or the emotional content of what they said rather than the exact words themselves. When recounting incidents out loud, we may narrate them with phrases like, "Then he said something about how I didn't need another pair of shoes. And I pointed out that he has, like, 500 pairs of shoes himself, and then he was just, UGH." This is clearly not a verbatim conversation. And, unless you specifically memorized the entire conversation, any attempt you have to repeat it word-for-word will result in your brain filling in some of the gaps with what it understood, rather than the actual words used.

So, given that our memories are more anecdotal than accurate, how can we trust ourselves to write an autobiography or a memoir?

I personally recommend being candid with your readers, as you would with any anecdote. In the autobiographical piece *Slash*, by Anthony Bozza and Slash of Guns 'n' Roses, the guitarist admits several times that the tale is told through his own lens and that others who witnessed certain events might have their own version to share.

Alternately, you can "screw your courage to the sticking place" and proceed with full confidence that you know exactly what you said, and you're willing to stand by it. Don't back down, and grit through any self-doubt with belief in your memories.

For the most part, this can only be troublesome if you start making up blatant lies about yourself. We live in the internet age, and it doesn't take too many keystrokes to discover that you did not, in fact, direct, write, and produce the blockbuster movie *Titanic*. Unless, of course, you are James Cameron, these are simply untrue claims.

There is a certain amount of humility that comes with writing about yourself. Sure, you have the power to spin and manipulate any conversation you've had into something that paints you as a hero. You can spend all the pages you wish justifying why you said what you said or did what you did. In fact, some people write memoirs for this exact purpose.

I can't dissuade anyone from putting on rose-colored glasses before they write about themselves, but consider how redecorating the "Halls of Memory" can benefit your reader. If you wash away all the stains of conflict, you might walk away looking pretty spiffy. But will your readers really understand the struggle and the lesson learned? No one really wants to read a book about things going really well all the time. They want the cathartic experience of tension building and being released. They want to learn lessons and understand things from a new perspective. Sure, they're interested in hearing about great people, but don't we all crave the truth? And sometimes, the truth gets a little gritty.

Before you commit to writing an autobiography or a memoir, ask yourself if you're okay writing about the things you may not love about your life. Are you ok with people you don't know reading about these things? What about people you do know, who may not be as familiar with those particular details of your life? If you feel any hesitation or reservation about these things, then maybe it's not time to write about it yet.

Many people write about themselves in order to share something they've gone through, either to give hope to others or to help themselves truly process the events and what they've learned as a result. When I share my personal experiences as a writer with you, I'm doing so to demonstrate that I've been in your position before, and to show you the roadmap of how I got through that particular challenge. I also recognize that most of my notes and early writing steps are messy, semi-incoherent, and often riddled with typos and errors. I could tidy that up before I commit it to the screen, but I prefer not to because I want you to appreciate that ugliness is part of the process. So many of us are caught up in the concept that we must do everything perfectly the first time, and that's simply impossible in writing. Rather than burn out on your first book trying to make things just right, I encourage you to slop around until you find your footing. If I show you my sloppiness, I hope that it makes you feel more comfortable with your own.

If your autobiographical piece includes some ugliness, be sure you're ready for it by preparing your notes. You are your own best resource here, but you can interview others. You can include actual historical events. You can paint yourself however you wish, but you can't make things up. And you're definitely going to make mistakes, but you have every chance to learn from it and come out of it looking not like a hero, but like someone readers can relate to.

To get a feel of how awkward or easy writing about yourself can be, let's give it a whirl for this chapter's writing exercise!

Exercise: 15 Minute Memoir

The premise of this exercise is exactly what it sounds like we're going to take 15 minutes out of our day to write a memoir.

As with exercises in my previous books, I'll be doing this alongside you and sharing what I came up with when I tried it myself. This means you get to read raw, unedited mind drivel in hopes that it will inspire you to make your own mess out of letters and words!

Supplies needed:
- *paper/writing utensil and/or open, blank .doc file, set to your preferences*

- *15 minutes of uninterrupted time*

- *optional - a timer to keep track of time*

As we just discussed, a memoir is an autobiographical piece that focuses on a specific event or occasion. That means you're going to spend the next quarter hour writing about one particular memory.

Step 1: Pick a Memory

I recognize that not everyone who is reading this book is absolutely sold on writing their own memoir, so let me give you a handful of topics to choose from:
- Your first day at a new school

- The first time you met your significant other

- A vacation or trip that you enjoyed a great deal

- Your favorite way to spend a summer afternoon

- A time when something embarrassing happened in front of your coworkers

- The first time you _____ (anything!)

For the purpose of this exercise, you don't necessarily have to make a major revelation or educate the audience. I encourage you to choose a topic that you'll feel comfortable brainstorming and writing about for the next 15 minutes. Don't choose anything emotional or that will require a deep dive into your psyche for this particular exercise—save that for the main event!

Step 2: Gather Your Wits

Before you get started, I recommend setting yourself up for success. This means setting a timer, getting your writing area organized, jotting down a few notes to help you keep on track, and placing a glass of water within convenient reach but not so close that you'll knock it over and interrupt yourself.

Close the doors, lower the blinds, tell everyone in your household to leave you alone, and get ready to write. If you need headphones or sound, make it happen now.

Step 3: Take a Deep Breath and Write

Clear your mind of any noise. Don't worry about messing up. Remember no one is going to actually read this. This is not a race. Don't worry about word count or typos. I'm not judging you.

Start the timer if you choose to have one, buckle up, and write.

Step 4: Stop and Read What You Wrote

Some writers—myself included—have to read what they've written immediately once they've stopped, or they'll never read it at all. It's really easy to assume that you've written something absolutely awful and procrastinate about reading it until you're so mortified by its existence, you delete it before you can read it and realize it really wasn't that bad.

Other folks like to take a break away from what they've just written so they can get out of their own heads. They reset their brain by focusing on something else so they can casually and peacefully approach their own material.

When it feels appropriate for you, take a look at what you came up with in those 15 minutes. Here's my effort, which should encourage you that perfection is not at all the point of this exercise:

My Very First Day of Kindergarten

When I attended kindergarten, it was still a half-day affair. You either joined the big kids on the bus in the morning when it was still dark and gray, or you got on the half-sized bus that cruised through the neighborhood on what we called "Baby Duty," dropping off the AM Kindergarten kids and picking up the afternoon shift.

I don't remember whether I was an AM or PM kid. I think it was afternoon, but I don't specifically remember. I do, however, remember that I stayed awake almost the entire night before my first day of kindergarten because I had no idea how this was going to shake out, and that made me feel scared.

My parents had informed me that if I was looking for someone to play with, a girl named Mindy would be a good choice because she lived in the neighborhood. That meant we could play more often. I asked why I hadn't met Mindy yet if she just lived up the street. My parents said I had, and I just didn't remember it.

It was still a few months from my fifth birthday when I started kindergarten. I had to take special tests and meet with people at the government buildings downtown. The tests were kind of fun—I had to think about the answers a bit. Talking to a bunch of strange grownups wasn't as much fun, but my parents told me it was okay to talk to them, so it wasn't exactly scary, either.

Whenever I finished a test or talked to someone, I got some paper and pens so I could draw for a bit. Unfortunately, this was the 1980s, so while my still-developing brain dreamed of creating an awe-inspiring portrait of Rainbow Brite, it was executed in standard office pen colors of red, green, blue, and black. I wondered why adults would bother being adults if they couldn't even draw in colors. "Maybe they should have crayons," I pondered as I scribbled my way through yet another juvenile noir take on a popular cartoon. I hoped kindergarten had crayons.

Kindergarten did, in fact, have crayons. It had bins upon bins of dusty halves and quarters of mutilated crayon stubs. Unlike the brand-new set of 36 that rested securely in a pocket strapped behind my seat, these abandoned nubbins were not organized by color, and while you could find a surprise like magenta or teal in there, it wasn't guaranteed. There was a distinct possibility that you might be coloring your entire page in shades of yellow and green. These were, in my personal estimation, the worst colors. Blue, purple, and orange were the best.

My kindergarten teacher was an actual saint of a grandmotherly woman. In my eyes, she was older than all of my grandparents combined. In reality, she was probably in her late 50s. She helped us find our seats and explained all of the different things in the classroom to us, and finally, finally, just before we were to go home, I got to meet Mindy.

As you read whatever arose to the surface of this exercise, ask yourself a few questions about what you wrote.

- Were you surprised by what memories you decided to focus on?

- Was this harder than you expected, or easier?

- Did you struggle to recall any particular facts?

- Do you think you could keep writing on this topic? (If so—go for it!)

For me, I was surprised by the fact that I remember how scared I was. I was fine with the idea of school, and even though I wasn't a socially inclined child, I knew how to entertain myself. It just felt like a really big commitment to something I didn't fully understand. It was interesting to see my brain walk through the process of how I became a kindergartner in this exercise.

The hardest part was trying to set the scene. I found myself writing as though I was talking to a kindergarten-aged me to give it a juvenile, simple feel. I would definitely edit this piece to more fully reflect that voice if I were to continue it. With more than 15 minutes at my disposal, I would have given more consideration to the voice and committed to it fully from the first word.

I couldn't remember whether I was an AM or PM kid. In fact, I probably spent at least one of my fifteen allotted minutes trying to remember. Consider this an argument for getting organized and coming up with ideas before you start writing because I could've used that minute to advance the actual story more.

I could probably keep writing about this, but I'd need to pare down the topic a bit more. Am I going to talk about how hard it was to establish new friendships? The frustrations of being an only child in a room filled with children who didn't share my passion for neatness and organization? A social piece on how we deprive office workers of creativity by only offering four basic colors of pen?

What I'm hoping to demonstrate with this exercise is all of the many things we've discussed in this chapter—from understanding the notable "characters" of biographical pieces to appreciating specific challenges that can arise when writing each type. I also hope you have an idea of how those concepts of choosing a shiny new topic, fine-tuning your perspective, and remaining organized can help you as you dive into your book.

You'll want to continue to keep these points in mind as we check out what it takes to write historical and travel-oriented books. Though the topics are very different, you are taking yourself out of your current context in order to write about people, times, and places that you may never experience firsthand. Some of what we have discussed about biographies will continue to serve you as we write about places, both in time and on the map.

HISTORY AND TRAVEL

B oth history and travel books are types of nonfiction that ask us to hop across dimensions in order to write our book. Though it is certainly possible to visit historic places, and travel destinations are limited by your budget and bravery, most historical and travel-related nonfiction are written from the viewpoint of someone who is currently in the time and place they are writing about.

There are, of course, exceptions. You may choose to write a travel diary, in which you capture your thoughts and actions while you are "on location," so to speak. Some could also argue that a diary is more of a memoir than a travel piece, which goes back to my earlier statement about nonfiction genres frequently blending and becoming a bit confusing.

For the sake of this chapter, we'll consider "historical pieces" as those which follow a specific event, a period in time, or a developmental process. Examples could include: "The Day Mount Vesuvius Erupted", "The Building of Native American Ceremonial Mounds in the Midwest", or "The Evolution of the Ford Mustang."

Travel pieces can have a lot of range, too, depending on your definition of "travel." Some writers focus on a particular location—let's use my father's hometown of Pawtucket, Rhode Island as an example. A book about Pawtucket could include a history of the location, notable residents, industry and commerce, places to eat, unique places to visit, local folklore and flavor, and nearby points of interest. It could also focus on a specific type of travel, such as "romantic getaways" or "fun for the whole family." You could even toe the line of history and write about what residents of Pawtucket did for fun between 1940 and 1970.

Other writers choose to highlight the process of traveling. Kristine Hudson is an author I admire greatly. Her books dance on the line between travel and how-to as she explains how she and her husband quit their jobs to live and work in a van. Your travel book may reflect on what you should pack, what to look for in an ideal vacation destination, when to choose side trips, and how to relax while getting ready to travel.

Then again, there's the experience of travel. Think of travel writer greats like Anthony Bourdain, who traveled the world to understand cultures through their cuisine, or Bill Bryson, who simply went for "A Walk in the Woods" and emerged with a best-seller. These writers take readers along for the journey, but they also pause and reflect on what their adventures mean, mentally, physically, and emotionally. While these books may have step-by-step guidebook elements, they often cross into autobiographical and memoir territory with their deep, introspective reflection.

There can even be an interplay between historical and travel-based pieces. If you're writing about a particular location, it's often helpful to get into historical notes when explaining points of interest. Let's say you're writing about things to do in Gettysburg. Aside from being a lovely spot in Pennsylvania, the battlefields are a significant part of local and American history. Someone writing a guide to the location would have a hard time avoiding a discussion about the Civil War and the importance of the "High Water Mark of the Rebellion."

Similarly, if you're discussing the history of a particular place, you might investigate what that place is really like. Every event occurred somewhere, and setting the scene is pretty important, as we'll discuss in a bit. For example, a book about Mount Vesuvius may include notes about places impacted by the eruption, such as Pompeii and Herculaneum. A description of the Italian coastline and where these places lie in relation to the volcano can help readers appreciate the impact of the eruption.

This is already a lot to think about, but rest assured that we're going to dive a lot deeper into creating your own historical or travel pieces. Take your time digesting this, and when you're ready, read on to take a look at some of the special considerations that writers of history and travel nonfiction may want to keep in mind.

Recognizing Rabbit Holes

When we are passionate about something, we tend to obsess about it. When we obsess about things, we often direct our energy into learning as much as possible and/or surrounding ourselves with the object of our passion. We build on our personal resources, developing our passion with knowledge. And just as every kettle needs to blow steam when it boils, we absolutely adore sharing our expertise when appropriate.

Great news! There is no time more appropriate than when you are writing your very own book about your favorite topic! However, just because you have a captive audience does not mean you should take this opportunity to hold them, hostage.

All writers explore rabbit holes—I'd say anyone with a certain level of curiosity is game to chase a concept through its entirety. If you've read *Alice's Adventures in Wonderland*, you may be familiar with what happens when you chase white rabbits down holes. While Alice truly did have an amazing experience, remember that she didn't enjoy all of it, and she encountered quite a bit of danger along the way. While you may be comfortably typing away in your seat, your future audience does not necessarily want to be taken on a wild ride.

Alternately, they may very much wish to go on a wild ride, but in a controlled and coherent sort of way. As the author, it is your responsibility to keep the reader entertained and informed, which means you have the power to wander through as many rabbit holes as you feel will help you explain your point. If there are too many rabbit holes, the infrastructure collapses, and if there are too few, your story will feel like a lateral shuffle through facts. Even scientific studies share related data and provide context.

Ultimately, your decision of what to include or not include in your book goes all the way back to the very first step, when you chose your shiny topic. In practice, however, you will find many shiny things along the way, and throughout your research, you might start to follow other authors' rabbit holes and get caught up in your own Wonderland adventure.

All types of nonfiction offer their own opportunities for intrepid researchers to get completely lost, disoriented, and re-routed. For some, this is a huge, distracting consumer of valuable time.

I don't want to say it's a "waste of time" because I feel we're never wasting time when we're learning and growing as human beings. However, I can say from experience that writing a book requires a certain level of energy. And while finding a new thread to research will provide fascination and a significant burst of endorphins, you may feel something akin to regret when you realize that you've spent all of your designated writing energy reading about something that really doesn't have anything to do with your book.

For some writers, though, this temporary lapse of focus is a blessing, because that rabbit hole led them away from their intended topic and into a new realm that's far more inspiring. Others, however, may be far too committed to their topic to switch gears and rearrange everything. I have experienced both of these scenarios, and they can be very emotional for so many reasons. I do recommend, if you find a particularly delicious diversion, to go ahead and take notes. Copy the resources so you can come back and possibly wrangle another book out of it. At the very least, you'll know where to start when you have time to research for fun again.

If you do decide to start over with this new information, I would also encourage you to not delete what you have so far. Your exploration thus far led you to this place, so it's possible you'll need to know how to make that journey again. Consider your research thus far a road map to opportunity, and save it for future voyages.

While all types of nonfiction are prone to writers diverging from the topic momentarily, historical

and travel pieces are particularly fertile grounds for off-topic exploration. My own theory is that there is simply such an abundance of moving pieces to analyze when you're looking at a historical event or describing something as generally exciting as travel. With so many glittering perspectives vying for your attention, it is very easy to get distracted by a particular element of your topic.

Again, this goes back to the stage where you worked to establish your perspective. This is why I recommend doing a lot of research at that stage before you jump in wholeheartedly. The more you feel comfortable with your topic and perspective, the less likelihood you'll have of encountering a new view that you'd rather explore. Not to say that hasn't happened to me many times, but sometimes it's less of a shock and more of a begrudging acceptance that your original topic wasn't as stellar as you thought.

What about research? Your research will help inform what you include in your nonfiction book, so you might want to pay close attention to how much your research and your book outline match. If you find yourself going off the rails frequently, then it's a good time to pause and really think about what you want to accomplish with this book. Sure, you've already assigned yourself a topic and perspective, and you probably have a good draft of an outline already. But what you've told yourself and what you really want are often two different things. And when you're writing a book because you want to write a book, you don't have to suffer. Unless you are on a deadline and money has exchanged hands, you don't *have* to write about anything. Even then, you might have a chance to present your new view in such a way that the client/editor/agent agrees with you!

You may have also noticed that I don't decry rabbit holes completely. I think a good wandering exploration can be handy in nonfiction pieces in order to keep them from becoming too straightforward. Understanding what life was like in Dearborn, Michigan when the first Ford Mustang rolled off the assembly line may not be super important to the evolution of the vehicle itself, but it can provide the reader with a valuable setting where they can rest while you explain the differences in manufacturing between the Dearborn plant of 1964 and the Flat Rock Assembly Plant, where the 2023 Ford Mustang was assembled.

As you practice writing, you'll become more accustomed to recognizing the sensation of falling down a rabbit hole. You'll eventually be able to rein in your research to focus strictly on the points you wish to make, and when writing, you'll eventually discover how to put the pieces together so that your heartfelt joy of sharing your knowledge is properly organized in the context of your book. Alternatively, your editors might kindly share this information with you before you get to the publishing stage, and you'll thank them profusely.

You're also probably starting to get a feel for how all of those things we covered at the beginning of this book—topic, perspective, and organization—can impact your overall writing experience. Not only are these things important for your audience, but I find that figuring these things out before I start writing—rather than bellyflopping onto the pages with aplomb—helps me stay calm and type, even when I'm feeling my least creative.

Now that we know what a rabbit hole is and how to recognize them, let's take a look at how adding detail to your book can actually make your book more valuable for the reader.

Recreating Another Place and Time

When you write a travel book, you take your readers to an entirely different place. They may have seen this place in person, or they may never visit. As a writer, your job is to explain this place to them in a way that allows them to picture it in their mind.

This, in itself, is a major challenge. When I write travel pieces, I'm reminded of the short story "Cathedral" by Raymond Carver. In the story, the author is enjoying a television program about cathedrals, and attempting to share this enjoyment with his wife's blind friend. I encourage you to read it in its entirety, but for the purpose of this example, consider how you would describe a place to someone who has never seen it and has no frame of reference for your description.

Sure, many of us can picture "relentless sunshine" or "mountains as far as the eye can see," but there's a difference between mustering up a decent mental picture and accurately capturing the way it feels when your horizon actually changes. Whether it's the multitude of emotions felt before a big voyage or the carnival of spices used on an unfamiliar local dish, you'll want to select just the right scenes to show your reader in order to fully capture the topic of your travel book.

Historical nonfiction adds yet another dimension to this equation: time. The very definition of historical means that the topic is in the past. Your readers therefore not only have to understand the location of your book, but the historical context, as well. This means educating them on not just the physical surroundings, but the cultural, socio-economical, educational, and religious context within the timeframe of your topic.

What you reveal, however, depends on your perspective. A book about Abraham Lincoln, for example, may or may not need to share his humble log cabin beginnings in order to make its point. Knowing what blue-collar workers in Dearborn did for fun may or may not relate to your examination of how horsepower has increased in the Mustang. On the other hand, it might be appropriate in a book about how trends and social cues have influenced the exterior appearance of the Mustang.

Historical and travel pieces tend to be more detail-oriented than other types of nonfiction, simply because there is so much stage to be set in order for the reader to follow along. As a writer, you'll have to decide which of the details are pertinent to your discussion.

At the very root of your decisions will be your topic, perspective, and organization. If your topic is suitably sized—not too narrow and not too nebulous—it will be much easier to determine what doesn't necessarily need a full poetic waxing and what deserves its own chapter. If you have a well-defined perspective, there will be some clear choices for additional discussion. And if you remain organized, you'll get a better intuitive feel for where all these pieces should fall in your book.

That being said, it takes a lot of practice to become proficient at this. If you revisit the "15 Minute Memoir" exercise, you'll likely notice a lot of parts that could probably be clipped or rearranged before you turned this into a book. You may realize that something you mentioned casually deserves a lot more attention, or that something doesn't necessarily belong anywhere. In my example, I'd definitely cut myself off when it came to the description of crayons. Though that was true and a part of the memory, it doesn't really have to do with the first day of kindergarten, my social awkwardness, or meeting Mindy.

As with rabbit holes, it's a "dealer's choice" situation as to where you direct the readers' attention with your writing. If you really want them to know about the bathrobe you used at the second AirBnB you stayed at, then go ahead and give that robe all of the attention it deserves. But as you're doing so, think of the reader, at home, wondering if that bathrobe is still there... heck, is the AirBnB still open?

As a new writer, I encourage you to just write. You can always remove things in editing, and tidy them up, so they relate more to the story. If you can recognize when your written recreation is becoming an actual rabbit hole and changing the course of your book, then you can avoid a lot of heartaches... but this skill is not always intuitive. You have to do what you think sounds best, you have to get lost a little bit, and you have to forge your own path back to reality, just like Alice. If you don't look at the past hundred words or so and ask yourself, "Wait! What am I doing?" at least a few times, then I envy you.

You are going to go down a few unnecessary rabbit holes, and you are going to find yourself adding unnecessary levels of detail like those decorative throw pillows that people have been obsessed with since the 1990s. You're going to look at your word count and realize that you just fired off 1500 words about late Victorian haberdashery when you were just trying to describe the hat that a British landlord's wife was wearing during the potato blight in order to highlight the role of classism in mass Irish emigration. Don't admonish yourself too harshly when this happens—instead, chalk it up to being part of the process, and if you like what you've written, save it somewhere before you delete it from this draft.

Author's Note: Do You Really, Really, Really Want to Write Nonfiction?

When it comes to recreating another place and time, we may be tempted to fill in the details we don't know with some ideas that we've invented. After all, how many readers can—or will—bother to verify these facts? (Answer: all of them.)

There is nothing more frustrating than having a blank spot on your canvas. As history writers, we often curse our ancestors for not keeping immaculate notes for us about absolutely everything. Presumably, the advent of social media will prevent future generations from ever wondering what we had for dinner, or what the view from the mezzanine looked like the night a show premiered on Broadway. But as for what we're writing now, we may still be waiting for archaeologists to discover the information that would fill in that blank space.

As a travel writer, it may be tempting to invent journeys that simply haven't happened. You can lie on a calm beach somewhere, watching paddleboarders skim across the sunset, and imagine the type of experience they're having. But the second you start to write about it like it's happening to you, you're no longer writing your own account. There may be a very valid reason why you aren't paddleboarding at that exact moment, but you can't accurately present that activity as your adventure.

There are ways around this. First, you can directly tell the audience that this is a blank spot and that you're filling it in with details based on your knowledge:

"While the details of the meetings have been lost to time, we know that Lee Laccoca's presentation must have been aggressive and exemplary, as the Mustang soon became Ford's top priority. Some speculate that he began with...."

"As I reclined on the beach, I couldn't help but imagine seeing the world through the eyes of the intrepid paddleboarders who passed silently between me and the setting sun. I could practically feel the...."

It's acceptable to admit that you don't know something. It's ok to share someone else's speculations with your audience, as long as you properly credit them.

It's also ok to write historical fiction. As we mentioned earlier, these are largely fictional tales based on actual historical events. It is entirely possible that your topic and perspective are best served at a fictional afternoon tea in which George Washington was in attendance, for example. Using what we know and painting a somewhat fictional world around it can be both informative and entertaining for audiences of all ages. You might be familiar with the novel *Gone with the Wind*. The events of the Civil War and Restoration Era described by Margaret Mitchell really happened, but Scarlett and Rhett weren't key players.

You may also want to consider writing a period piece. In this type of fiction, most of the elements are fictional but take place in a specific time and place. *The Great Gatsby* is an example of a period piece, in that it is a social message specific to The Roaring '20s, but the people, places, and events are all fictional. There is a fine line between historical fiction and period pieces, but that more or less comes down to how your book is marketed. As long as you're not trying to pass fiction off as nonfiction, you're doing everything correctly.

Travel-based fiction is also a thing! I truly appreciate this definition of "Travel Narrative," as provided by Benjamin Colbert in The Encyclopedia of Romantic Literature, 2012:

Travel writing is widely considered a hybrid genre, fusing factual reportage with fictional technique, on-the-spot observation with recollections in tranquility, scientific detail with poetic allusion, and verbal description with a visual illustration.

One of the more famous pieces in this genre would arguably be Jack Kerouac's "On the Road." Based on an actual road trip, this novel explores the meaning of life, and whether freedom is possible. Considered one of the significant creations from the Beat Generation, it's a story, social commentary, and a travelogue, all packed together.

Choosing to add the element of fiction to your historical or travel book can be a fantastic, complex opportunity. You'll not only research the facts, but you'll also get to invent your own elements as well!

At the risk of relentless self-promotion, I do encourage readers who are interested in fiction writing to check out my earlier books, especially *One Word at a Time*, which specifically focuses on the fiction-writing process. If at any time it feels like I'm going too fast, it's likely because I'm trying to not be too repetitive.

Now that we've looked at how to recognize rabbit holes, being true to all dimensions of the setting, and determining how much reality is going to direct your writing, it's time to put it all together and take your reader to your topic.

Taking Them There

Picture this: You're at home, curled up in bed. You're wearing your favorite comfy clothes, and you've got a beverage sitting beside you that's exactly perfect for the occasion. You're reading a book, and despite the fact that you are physically holed up in a Minnesota snow squall, the book you're reading about Hawaii has you feeling warm and carefree.

If you've ever had a chance to really dwell on the concept, you may recognize that the human imagination is a very strange thing. Our brains have this function that allows us to take written descriptions and turn them into nearly tangible experiences. With just the right words, we can smell the food cooking in the marketplace, hear the cacophony of voices on the lawn just before the President begins to speak, and feel the gentle grit of sand on the soles of our feet.

But I just told you to be wary of rabbit holes, and we've discussed fine-tuning details to those that are factual and necessary. So how are you supposed to take your reader with you through space and time?

Taking your readers where they need to be in order to really experience the topic from your perspective is the top challenge for all writers. There is a sweet spot between brevity and verbosity. There are such things as "too much" and "too little," but your ability to paint a picture for your reader is limited only by what you're willing to put on the canvas.

And like painters, writers have different styles. Despite being contemporaries, Ernest Hemingway and F. Scott Fitzgerald would likely describe the very same glass of absinthe in very different ways. Perhaps the glass, the lighting, the piano playing in the background, or the liquid itself would be the most important, depending on the perspective.

If you are new to the art of writing, you likely don't have an established style yet. This means you'll still find yourself wondering where the "just right" spot is when it comes to detail and description. My advice is to stick with it, keep writing, and read what you've written from time to time to make sure you're sticking to your intended structure.

No one has written the "perfect" book that makes every reader happy, and it's unlikely to happen. What you can do, however, is write the very best book that you can write, right now, given what you've got in terms of experience and knowledge. Your style will develop as time goes by, and you'll get better at seeing when you're about to wander off-topic, and when you're giving the readers exactly the right demonstration of place and time.

When I say "taking them there," I mean allowing your reader to use their imagination to escape their current surroundings and experience the time and place of your book. This can be as simple as adding a few adjectives to a sentence or spending a few extra sentences describing how the scene would be interpreted by the five senses.

Luckily, we have an abundant array of luscious, poignant, pointed, abrupt, bold, flowery, and otherwise descriptive words to help us along our journey. I encourage you to use them at your leisure for your readers' pleasure (and your own).

Let's take a look at a few examples and practice this effect ourselves with this chapter's exercise.

Exercise: The Importance of Show vs. Tell

I am admittedly a huge devotee of show and tell. From the days of holding my favorite stuffed toy high above my head and explaining to my entire kindergarten class how very much Felix the Pumpkin meant to me, to the present day, in which I get to show and tell for a living, I have always adored delivering picturesque descriptions and plain directions.

So, if you're wondering if this is another Lauren Bingham show/tell exercise, I assure you it is. This one is unique, however, in that we're going to focus on a nonfiction topic.

Supplies needed:
- *paper/writing utensil and/or open, blank .doc file, set to your preferences*

- *Your "muse"*

Step 1: Behold Your Muse

I'm calling it a "muse" to be witty, but we're going to need some external support for this one. Find a photo or painting of a place and time that is not here and now. Anything will suffice for this exercise, such as:

- A selfie you took on vacation last year

- A portrait of a famous figure

- A landscape photograph

- A picture of a building you're familiar with

Don't stretch too far or try too hard to find something. The more familiar you are with the picture you choose, the more natural this exercise will feel, but you can do this with a picture of a place or time you've never experienced before.

Step 2: Observe Your Picture

Start jotting down notes about what you see in the photo. They don't have to be coherent or even particularly descriptive. For example, let's say I've chosen a photo I took in 2001 of two of my friends standing in front of the Chicago skyline.

I might start with:

- *It's dark*

- *It's clearly cold outside—people are wearing coats*

- *There's a little bit of snow on the rocks*

- *They're by the lakefront*

- *The city is in the distance, but still recognizable*

Step 3: Tell Me What's in the Picture

Even though the phrase is "show and tell," I find it more helpful to start with the telling, and add the show from there. You may feel differently, in which case, it's perfectly fine to swap this step with Step 4.

Essentially, you're going to tell an imaginary audience about what is in the picture. Whether it's an important dignitary or a little-known spot you visited long, long ago, connect with the picture long enough to tell your reader what's going on.

In my case:

This is a picture of my friends Shaquan and Vickie. It was taken during a trip to Chicago in December 2001. The weather was snowy, and we didn't have much money, so we took a walk after dinner and stopped to take this picture with a disposable camera in Uptown with the city lights in the background.

Not bad. A "telling" description is direct, without added color commentary. You've got just enough adjectives to know the who, where, what, when, and how of the scenario. There's nothing wrong with this approach, and there are many cases where "telling" the audience about a scene in a brief and fact-driven manner is appropriate.

Step 4: Show Me What's in the Picture

In this step, we're going to create our own version of the photograph using words. I want you to go all out here. No corner of the picture is off-limits. I want to read about this photograph in words so glorious, so vivid, that I can't help but get a mental picture. In fact, try to get as many senses as possible involved so you can really take anyone reading your description to the scene.

Back to Chicago:

December in Chicago is generally cold, damp, and depressing, though not necessarily in that order. On the night of our visit, we were all feeling a bit grumpy, and the oppressive moist wind that constantly blows by the lake isn't exactly refreshing when your shoes are full of snow.

Still, our spirits were high. We'd just finished off a tasty dinner at the taqueria down the street from our host Shaquan's tiny studio apartment. We'd soaked in the warmth and the most delicious horchata in Uptown before heading out into the darkness. Without too many pennies to our names, our best form of entertainment was walking.

We didn't make it far. The whipping wind, the fullness of our bellies, and the desire to be anywhere that wasn't cold and damp led us to turn around once we got to the lake.

Before we continued our trudge back to the apartment, though, Vickie begged us to take a quick picture of her with the lake and skyline. She asked Shaquan to pose with her, since he had been so kind to host us, and he obliged. Together, they stood with cheeks shiny and pink from the cold, noses dripping, coats disheveled, with the lights of the city glowing radiantly behind them.

Again, this is raw footage, so to speak, so I wouldn't say I followed my own advice here. I didn't mention what they were wearing, what we ordered at the taqueria, our exact path to the lake, and so on.

But, as I've said several times, there's no wrong answer, just as there is no "right" way to do these exercises. What I hope you notice when reading both of your samples is that telling is a much more straightforward type of writing, while showing is more descriptive and often more immersive for your reader.

Here's the tricky part: writing a book that is strictly telling or strictly showing is absolutely exhausting for the author and the reader. Instead, it's best to apply each method in just the right dose. But even worse—there's no golden equation that tells you how much showing and/or telling you should do.

Your personal style will dictate a great deal of how much "flower and spice" you put into your writing. Additionally, some topics lend themselves to detail more readily than others. A 2x4 plank and a 240-year-old tree are not going to provide the same level of fascination or word count.

When I'm trying to decide how much creativity I want to spill onto these pages, I often try to put myself in the position of my reader. Does it make sense to go into deep descriptive detail here? Does it really matter if Shaquan was wearing a green plaid shirt and Vickie was wearing my orange sweater? If I am trying to actually take the reader into that scene, then yes. If I'm trying to be informative of simple facts, then maybe not.

So how do you decide if it's time to take the reader into the scene or whether being informative of simple facts is more appropriate?

Immersing the reader in the scene and putting them in that place and time so completely that they lose track of their current location requires dedication, patience, and impressive powers of observation. If you're the kind of person who gets emotional at the beauty of morning dew on the grass, this type of writing can be pretty intuitive to you.

Informing the reader of facts isn't necessarily as simple as it sounds, either. There's really no such thing as an "event" so much as there are "many things that happened in an increasingly less random way that led up to this event." When writing a history or travel book, it can be very tempting to go into "And Then" mode:

"Then the Beatles decided to go to America. And then they took a plane across the Atlantic Ocean, and then they landed in New York. And then there were a bunch of people waiting for them at the airport."

"Then we went back to the hotel, and then we took a shower and just hung around while we waited for our dinner reservations. And then we took an Uber to the restaurant. It was good. And then we went back to the beach."

"And Then" mode is safe. It's easy. It gets to the point very quickly. But don't you have a few questions when you read those snippets? Don't you want to know just a little bit more?

So how do you go about writing some of the most descriptive nonfiction genres without losing your audience? Patience. Practice. All of the three tenets of "'Good' Nonfiction" as discussed in the first chapter. But mostly practice.

If you intend to publish your pieces, rest assured that your readers will cheerfully tell you exactly what they think of your style. What you do with that information is entirely up to you. I personally like to digest each critique or compliment individually. If I start noticing trends in either column, I'll know that I've got something to work on, or that I've found a sweet spot.

Furthermore, critiques and compliments are just the opinions of one person. Some people like saying nasty things for fun, especially on the internet. Nearly everything I've published has at least one review that was clearly written just to get laughs at my expense. Honestly, I think it might be a lower form of flattery since people have to actually purchase and read my books in order to bloviate about how much they hated it.

Ultimately, you get to decide how you take your readers to the place and time in which your history or travel book takes place. You can go down all the rabbit holes, do all of the research to fill in the blanks, use all the adjectives, and do just as much showing and telling as your heart desires. You can't decide how your readers will react or how much they'll enjoy it, but you do get to choose how much you let that information impact your life and writing style.

Just keep writing, and before long, your style will start to feel more familiar and automatic. Trust me—I write "how-to" books about it!

This brings us to our next nonfiction genre: self-help and how-to books. It's time to tie these two books into our nonfiction fundamentals to create a strong book that provides the intended level of guidance.

SELF-HELP AND HOW-TO

S elf-help and how-to books are often a bit of a delicate area simply because every human is different, and each of us likes to be told what to do in different manners. And, when you write a self-help or how-to book, you are absolutely telling people what you think they should do.

As someone who has penned quite a few "how-tos" and even a couple of self-help workbooks, I will loudly admit that these are some of the hardest to write, emotionally. I know—that is to say, I expect, understand, and fully acknowledge—that someone is going to read my how-to books and say "That's not how you do it at all! How dumb is this writer?"

In fact, there are infinite ways to focus on and better ourselves, just as there is more than one way to skin a knee (to make an old phrase more palatable).

When writing these types of books, you have to be aware that there are people who have found and are extremely comfortable with their own methods. I enjoy having discussions with others in which we share our differing views and processes because you can learn a lot about yourself when you consider other perspectives. Some people are not as open to discourse. These people will still purchase, read, and unilaterally hate your self-help or how-to book at some point.

So, if your motivation for writing one of these books is to be "right" and make everyone realize they've been doing it terribly wrong their entire lives, you will be sincerely disappointed. Forming a cult or changing the world is often more than a one-book effort.

Instead, I like to think of writing guidance books as an option for those who are seeking assistance around a particular topic. I don't claim to be *the* answer, but merely an option. I ask readers to take inspiration from my text, rather than proclaiming it the "only" way.

You have to have a certain amount of confidence to write a guidance book. Some writers are absolutely positive that what they're sharing with their audience is going to revolutionize their way of thinking. Others are hoping to join the conversation on a topic with what they feel is a valid point to make. Most fall somewhere in between.

To put it plainly: readers like to know that their author knows what they're talking about. As they peruse your text, they want to feel assured that you're not just making it up as you go along. Especially in the case of self-help and how-to books, readers want to know that they are following a trusted authority.

In order to do that, you'll want to be a guiding force for your readers. You'll want to come from a place of helping and assistance. Furthermore, you'll want to present your ideas in a way that your reader understands and can follow. And, as you're probably guessing, a lot of that comes down to topic, perspective, and organization.

Let's take a look at the nonfiction principles in action here.

Being the Guiding Hand

For the purpose of this chapter, I'm going to continue under the assumption that you are writing a self-help or how-to book with the intention of others reading it. It's not a requirement, of course, and you're free to hide your book from humanity forever. However, folks don't generally write these types of books if they want to keep the contents a secret. Therefore, the chapters in this chapter will assume deliberate interaction with the reader.

When you're considering writing a self-help or how-to book, there are a few questions you should ask yourself before you get too invested in this project:

- Why do you want to write this book?

- Who are you writing this book for and who do you want to read and follow it?

- Why would someone choose this book over all of the other books on this topic?

- What are you trying to accomplish or what do you hope to be the result of writing this book?

It's okay to be a tiny bit egotistical here. For the most part, the main reason anyone wants to write a guidance book is because they've discovered a method, process, or point of view that is helping them and they wish to share it with others. Approach your book with the understanding that your thoughts are valid, helpful, and worth sharing. Admitting that not everyone will agree with you is an exercise in humility, but once you've become accustomed to this concept, you can write on with the knowledge that your book is worth reading.

That being said, there are things you can do as an author to make the journey as comfortable as possible for your readers.

Once you've identified your motivation behind writing this book, it's time to review your choice of topic and perspective in light of your realizations. Once again, you'll ask yourself the timeless question authors have agonized over since the first written word: "Does this make sense?"

It is highly likely that you'll look at all of the notes and thoughts you've accumulated and feel your throat tighten, your heart starts beating a little faster, and your stomach flip-flops a bit. That's normal. Many people are uncomfortable with stepping into the role of an authority figure, so feeling a little overwhelmed is natural. On top of that, you're likely looking at a whole mess of ideas, and it may not seem like they have any connection to each other. You may be wondering if you just wasted a significant amount of time making an overwhelming mess that you'll have to abandon before it drives you mad.

While you may ultimately decide to start over, this moment of anxiety doesn't necessarily mean you've done it all wrong. Instead, consider this an opportunity to really spend some time with your notes and your topic. You wouldn't have jotted down all of these spur-of-the-moment thoughts if they didn't have some sort of meaning to you.

This may be a great opportunity to start categorizing and organizing your notes. You may have a lot of material on one aspect—a rabbit hole, perhaps—so take the time to put all of the relevant details, links, quotes, and resources together. Come up with a label for each category of notes, such as "Scientific Studies Related to (Topic)," "Historical Facts," or "Step-by-Step Procedures."

This brings me to the next point—writing a guidance book does not exempt you from doing research. Part of filling the role of the "Trusted Authority" means really and truly knowing what you're talking about.

You are the expert on your own self-help or how-to methods, concepts, and processes, but you do need to have some actual facts in there. If you were to write a book on how to change your furnace filter, for example, you would benefit from knowing about the world of filter options, different types of furnaces, why changing a furnace filter is important, the risks of neglecting to do so, and when to contact a professional. You don't necessarily have to cover all of these topics in your book, but being able to confidently and factually explain your recommendations in context will help your reader believe in your credibility.

This is also true for self-help books. If your goal is to help someone change their life, it's a good idea to back your ideas with facts about how making these adjustments can actually benefit them. Sharing the consequences of continuing their behavior can help them appreciate why shifting their perspective might be necessary. Scientific facts, anecdotal evidence, and understanding the theories behind certain behaviors can be helpful as you coax your readers into considering a different process.

I have gone as far as enrolling in courses through community colleges or online learning platforms to make sure I have the right level of confidence to commit to and complete a book. You don't necessarily have to get an advanced degree in your topic, but having a solid background will help you build credibility both as an author and in the text you create.

So, as you're putting everything together, and wondering why you're doing this, and if any of your decisions make sense, consider also how much research you've put into your topic. Doing a little investigation as you ponder your topic can truly help you narrow down your perspective as a guidance book writer, as well. Once again, topic, perspective, and organization weave together to create the net that will guide your book to shore, metaphorically speaking.

Stepping into the role of the "guiding hand" when writing a self-help or how-to book is a little more involved than slapping down a few ideas on paper. You need to connect with the reader as a trusted authority. This may mean taking a good, long look at your motivation, as well as doing any additional research to truly know what you're talking about. Focusing deeply on your topic from a "why and how" angle can help you settle into this role quite nicely.

You'll also want to consider what type of helper you want to be, so let's explore the importance of tone in a self-help or how-to book.

How to Be a Helper

We talked about how your style can impact the overall outcome of your book in the last chapter, but there's a slight difference between your style and your tone. While they do essentially work in tandem, your style refers to the types of words you use, the length of your sentences, the particular adjectives and adverbs you incorporate, and how you weave together your paragraphs. Your tone, on the other hand, directly implies the voice you use when writing your book.

When reading my books, I hope you find the tone lighthearted and friendly. I don't want to come across as a bully. I don't want to pretend I am the only beacon of knowledge in the art of writing. I don't want there to be anything forceful or uncomfortable about my books because in my opinion, writing a book is hard enough without someone barking premonitions of failure towards you.

However, if I were writing about a more dire topic, such as "How to Quit Smoking" or "Overcoming Agoraphobia through Basic Lifestyle Changes," I would likely choose a more serious and straightforward tone. The world will not stop turning if you take five years to write a book. The consequences of tobacco use or facing a major psychological challenge are far more important. (Please note that I say all of this with no judgment towards those who engage in tobacco use or are experiencing major psychological challenges—we all have our things to deal with in our own way!)

Ultimately, the tone of your book is once again your own choice. No one is going to stop you from writing exactly the book you want to write.

That being said, if you are interested in finding a way to be a helper, I encourage you to take the time to explore the tone you intend to use when writing your book.

Your perspective is going to take center stage here. If you're writing from the point of view that the reader desperately needs to follow your advice or bad things will happen, it's more likely that you'll take a direct, no-nonsense tone with lots of wording like "you must," "you will," and "you need to." For example:

If you want to write a nonfiction book, you must put your nose to the grindstone and follow the steps I provide. You will find yourself extremely confused and lost if you don't. You need to understand the consequences of being disorganized and wishy-washy with your topic. I guarantee you'll regret not following my instructions!

Alternately, if you're trying to gently coax someone into the preparation stages of behavior modification, you might take a lighter approach:

Modern science isn't sure why some people feel compelled to write books. But if you find yourself wondering what it would take to write a nonfiction book, then perhaps it's time to consider what the process entails in order to help you decide whether this is something you should try.

So how do you decide? I'm so very glad you asked. Let's look a little deeper at your audience, and what they need from you as the writer of a guidance book.

Author's Note: Connecting with Your Nonfictional Audience with Your Nonfiction Writing

Do you remember way back in Chapter 1, when we thought about who would potentially read our book? Whether or not you went as far as researching demographics, or simply attempted to picture an actual person with your book in their hand, hopefully, you've taken the time to consider who your audience is.

I recommend revisiting the notes you made on this topic from the first exercise and comparing them to your responses to the "Why do you want to write this book" questions from the last chapter.

Look for any discrepancies. If you said you want to write your book to "reform existing bad behavior," but you want your book to be read by young children, you're going to have to really consider how you're going to convince your audience that they're being naughty, but that they can become good children if they just follow your advice.

Likewise, if you're writing a how-to book, consider how much experience your reader has with the topic at hand. Are you writing for absolute beginners, folks who have tried and failed, or those who are near-experts trying to get to the next level?

Knowing who you're writing for will help inform the language and vocabulary you use, as well as your tone. Weaving together your tone with your perspective and style may seem like a daunting task, especially if you're not a well-seasoned author. To be honest, there have been times when I've halted typing in frustration and shouted, "I don't know how to talk to you!" because I found myself sliding into a totally unintended voice.

It is possible to experience difficulty when writing to a particular audience. It may be stressful and uncomfortable to use a tone that isn't your standard way of speaking. You may need to reconsider whether or not you have selected the right audience for you.

Any time you start to get flustered and feel reality spinning away from you, pause. Clear your mind. Take deep breaths or perform mindfulness exercises. There will be days when you'll cheerfully bang out 3,000 words before you finish your morning coffee, and there will be days when you don't get any writing done because you're busy untangling yourself from the knot you've written yourself into. Finding yourself in a predicament doesn't mean you've gone wrong—it just means you need to trace yourself back to where things started to veer off track and figure out the best way to either get back on a course or build a new path.

In order to connect with your audience, you need to not only know what you're talking about, but who you're talking to in the first place. This can be difficult in nonfiction writing because you don't always have sympathetic characters for the reader to love or familiar situations for them to identify with. Instead, you have a bunch of facts that you wish to impart, and in the case of self-help and how-to books, you're trying to actively help them change paths and do things in a specific way.

I encourage you to take your time but don't allow yourself to obsess over whether your tone is exactly right at all times. Your top priority should be getting through the draft. Yes, you should keep yourself in check and stay on topic, keep your perspective even, and remain diligently organized so that you can maintain all of the various "dos and don'ts" that we've addressed so far. But if you turn your brain inside-out trying to make a perfect first draft, you'll quickly become miserable. And while artists of all types are known for suffering for their art, you don't actually have to. It's not a requirement, but if you find yourself experiencing melancholia, insufferable torture, or spending an extraordinary amount of time languishing or lamenting, you're in good literary company. Stay calm; write on.

Edits are always possible. Even something as deeply embedded into every syllable like your tone can be altered and adjusted after you've finished your first draft. It might not be the ideal situation, but neither is melancholia and lamentation. Proceed with your draft with your sanity as a priority.

My advice for those who are attempting to connect with an audience they've never met is to focus on being genuine. Sure, you may need to fine-tune the verbiage in the editing stage, but if you're authentically passionate about your topic, you will frequently succeed in sounding exactly like the trusted authority your reader is hoping for.

As we're working on some of the finer points of our voice and style, let's drill down a bit into the finer points of organization, as well. Guiding people means keeping them on the right path. And to do that, you'll need to make sure the path is clear and inviting. Let's find out how.

How to How-To

When writing your self-help or how-to book, I highly recommend considering your readers' level of exposure or expertise with the topic and adjusting the format and pacing of your explanation accordingly.

Reflecting on the demographic and perspective you've chosen; carefully consider how much knowledge you're going to need to pack into your chapters. Imagine that when your readers pick up your book, they're being dropped off at the starting point of a brand-new journey. Everyone is going to arrive with their own experiences, challenges, preferences, and opinions.

As the writer, it's your job to figure out what type of guide you're going to be. Where does your readers' journey begin? How are you going to welcome them and get them orientated to your methods and processes? What are you going to do to position them for success?

Again, you'll want to consider how aggressive or gentle you wish to be with your readers. You'll want to consider their skill and comfort level. And while it would be impossible to accommodate every reader, you've already taken the time to carefully select a demographic and perspective and whittled down your topic to best express your thoughts to this chapter of the population. Right?

When writing a self-help or how-to book, you're going to need to first explain to yourself how you're going to lead your reader down this new and exciting path. Consider yourself a tour guide. What steps or features are you going to highlight? How much background information do you want to give your readers to ensure they understand the situation or processes at hand?

What methods do you think will best help them grasp your concepts? I like to include aside "Author's Note" chapters and exercises to engage my readers, along with a Resources chapter to provide you with additional information on topics that I might have skimmed over a bit more than readers wanted. You don't have to use these specific techniques for your own book, but take time to think of any additional steps you can take to help enhance your audience's comprehension and absorption of your book.

You might want to play around with the different steps you provide to your readers. Consider a ramp and a staircase. They both do the same job of allowing folks to travel up or down a change of elevation. A ramp, however, allows those using it to choose how much space they cover as they move. Stairs, on the other hand, require users to take equally sized steps in order to complete their journey. As a writer, you can choose between giving your readers a ramp or stairs, depending on the level of detail you provide and how you provide it.

When attempting to take your audience from Point A to Point B, a linear format is often the most direct path. That doesn't mean you won't have a few rabbit holes leading away from the main path, as we discussed, but rather that you'll start at the beginning and finish the book with the knowledge that will change your readers' lives, perspectives, and skill sets. This format often includes several regimented steps that logically build on each other.

The ramp method of guidance is most apparent in the pacing of your book. If you're writing a book about mindfulness exercises for an experienced audience, you don't need to start with the basics of meditation, breathing, and body scanning. You might acknowledge them and build a ramp over them allowing you to advance quickly to the actual instruction.

How do you do this? Pacing is a great way to keep your readers marching through your piece at the correct tempo. "Pacing" refers to the amount of thought and words you devote to each concept in your book, and how rapidly you transition from idea to idea. On top of that, the words you choose and your sentence structure can establish a rhythm that can break down your thoughts into bite-sized pieces or help your reader cruise up a ramp to the next big consideration. You may notice that my sentences get a bit shorter when I'm trying to make a point that I feel is important. On the other hand, when I want to delight you into remembering and digesting the information I've shared, I'll bloviate a bit with whimsy and self-reflection.

Let's try an exercise to help establish a feel for how-to. After all, practice is the best way to fine-tune your style and help you appreciate the interplay between all of the painstaking moving pieces that make a successful guidance book!

Exercise: Before We Walk, We Crawl

When we're telling someone how to do something or how to reconsider their current situation, we often use a step-by-step approach to the process. I've done this for all of the exercises in this book so far.

A step-by-step approach takes its name from the basic staircase. You start on the ground floor with no knowledge, then take a step "up" as you gain more knowledge, until at long last, you've reached the next level of mastery. Each step builds upon what you learned in the last one in an obvious, sequential, equally measured manner.

A linear process to guiding readers to their goals is often simpler for them to follow. Consider your own reading habits to help you appreciate the perspective of your future readers. Most of us have quite a bit going on in our lives, and being able to keep track of which stage of the process we're in will help us stay focused on incorporating your methods into our lives.

In this exercise, we'll approach a process in a step-by-step manner. We'll assume that the reader has so little understanding of the topic that they only picked up your book in order to figure out whether the title was in a make-believe language.

Supplies needed:

- *paper/writing utensil and/or open, blank .doc file, set to your preferences*

- *15 minutes of uninterrupted time, with or without a timer*

Step 1: Choose Your Process

You can decide to write about any activity you want, but here are a few sample topics to help you get started with the brainstorming process:

- How to ride a bike

- How to whistle

- How to wash a car

- How to make the perfect cup of tea/peanut butter and jelly sandwich/casserole

- How to change the toilet paper roll when it's empty, surely, I'm not the only person who possesses this amazing skill

Make sure that the activity has enough steps to warrant 15 minutes of writing. Otherwise, you'll be desperately filling in the time with nonsense and fluff. Likewise, don't choose a topic that requires several volumes of detailed explanation. This is just a 15-minute writing exercise.

Step 2: Outline Your Steps

Take a few moments to consider the steps involved in the process you're about to explain. Think of the very first thing a person must do in order to take this journey. What preparation is necessary? Then skip forward to what the reader should be able to accomplish when they're done with your instructions. What does success look like?

Now your job is to fill in the steps between "Start" and "Finish." Make some notes to sketch out some of the steps you'll highlight in your exercise.

Step 3: Set the Timer and Start Writing!

Once you're relatively comfortable with the outline you've created, it's time to start writing. Here's what I came up with on the topic of "How to Turn on My Computer:"

While technology has come to unite humanity, it turns out that our tech devices are as different as two humans can be, despite having no sentient attachments.

Most folks turn on their computers by pressing a button or two. I press a button or twelve, depending on what I'm doing wrong on any given day.

I've been assured that the correct method is to first assure that both the monitor and the laptop are plugged into the power strip. In order to streamline this process, I've looped red tape around the monitor cord and green around the laptop's cord. I can easily tell if they're plugged in.

The next step is to make sure the cats haven't unplugged any of the cords that tether the monitor, the laptop, and the router to each other like digital castaways. This is slightly more difficult because I ran out of color-coded tape. However, the cords are so tangled, that a light jiggle of any cable will make all of them wiggle, but only if they're plugged in correctly.

Now it's time to start pressing buttons. I like to start with the monitor button, though it really doesn't matter where you start. You'll be pushing everything a few times.

The first time you push the monitor button, it will pop to life in a blaze of white and purple streaks. This is a farce. Turn it off and roll your eyes. Don't believe the lies. After you've counted to 10, press the monitor power button yet again. Nothing will happen. Count to 10 again, and it will splash to life as if nothing has happened with the warning "No Device Detected."

Again, we know this to be false, since we jiggled and wiggled the cords. It's time to engage the laptop itself.

Open the laptop. If the screen remains blank for more than 30 seconds, close the laptop again. Open it again. It should sputter and flash and eventually cough up your screen. Close the laptop. Take a few moments to make sure you're comfortable, have a glass of water, put your phone on the charger, or go to the bathroom. When you return, you should finally have my laptop in full, upright, functioning order.

Step 4: Read What You've Written to See What You've Missed

Since this was a timed writing exercise, it is fairly likely that you didn't include some pertinent details in your step-by-step process. Looking at my own writing, I see I've neglected to mention that the laptop is calmly awaiting your attention on top of my desk. I told the reader to open and close it, but I didn't tell them where to find it or what it looked like.

When you reread your how-to steps, take into account how much detail you've used in each step of the process. Can someone who is reading these directions for the first time visualize or identify all of the moving parts? Are your instructions specific enough for them to follow along?

If you tell someone to, "take a deep breath," for example, are you asking them to take a single deep breath, or do you actually want them to take as many deep breaths as it takes to clear their mind? What type of deep breathing technique do you want them to use? Slow counting inhale? Forceful exhale? Through the mouth or the nose?

Some details can be glossed over–for example, when I explain you'll need a piece of paper or a blank computer document. I'm going to assume that you know what paper looks like and/or how to use your devices. Don't patronize your readers, but recognize that everyone has a different starting point. Everyone has a different understanding of their world, and some folks have more questions than others.

If you leave your reader with too many questions, you'll likely lose their interest after a while. If you have too many gaps in your instructions, your audience will simply stop trying to follow after the first time they get lost.

I encourage you to have someone else read your exercise, too. Ask if they would feel confident following these steps, and what types of questions they have about the process. Ask them if the format is clear, and whether you need to slow down or speed up your steps. Are these appropriate, even baby steps, or are you asking them to tiptoe to the base of the hill, and then run up it as fast as they can?

Most folks are hesitant to try new things. The prospect of failure is terrifying. In most cases, it's much easier for all of us to just not do the new thing instead of trying and flailing around with wild incompetence as we try to learn. But as self-help and how-to writers, it is quite literally our duty to encourage people to try and to set them up not necessarily for ultimate success, but at least with the confidence that they can get through the book without feeling attacked, frustrated, or confused. Suffice it to say that readers who feel attacked, frustrated, or confused do not leave happy reviews, nor do they continue to purchase your books.

Writing guidance books such as self-help and how-to pieces can be a bit nerve-wracking. As the writer, you are accepting responsibility for taking your reader on a potentially life-changing voyage. But to do that, you must be a sympathetic and trustworthy guide. How you approach your audience, the tone you use, and the manner in which you take your audience through the process can help them believe not only in you but in the book you've written.

PHILOSOPHY AND INSIGHT/ANALYSIS

We're going to spend less time discussing the last two nonfiction genres. This is not because they are any less important, complicated, or deserving of discourse but because we're taking this chapter as an opportunity to pull together everything we've learned so far.

In each chapter so far, we've looked at different types of nonfiction and examined the three major concepts that form the roots of "good" nonfiction:

- Choosing a topic that isn't too narrow or broad

- Finding a perspective that is unique, informative, and entertaining

- Organizing not only the book itself but also your research

From there, we've wandered through a metaphorical garden of nonfiction touchpoints and techniques:

- Accuracy and your mission as a fact-finder

- Avoiding possible legal woes

- Achieving the right level of detail for your audience

- The importance of background information, related threads, and other "rabbit holes"

- Options for those who wish to explore the line between fiction and nonfiction

- The choice between taming and igniting your descriptive text

- Refining your formatting, tone, and pacing to provide your audience with the most relatable content

We've woven all of these pieces together into a complicated fabric that may more resemble a cobweb than a tapestry at this point. Once again, I urge you to be brave and charge on, confident that one way or another, you'll end up with a first draft of some sort.

Our last two nonfiction genres to cover are philosophy and insight books. These two book types have somewhat of a nebulous definition when it comes to the material covered and how it's structured. In fact, there are some resources that consider these subcategories of self-help books.

Ultimately, these books are written to reveal your individual perspective on a certain topic. If you are offering this perspective with the intention of adjusting the reader's understanding of existence, you are likely writing a philosophy book. If you're writing for the sheer purpose of making your readers aware of your thoughts, opinions, understanding, and conclusions derived from your studies on a topic, this would be considered an insight or analysis book.

Like every type of nonfiction, we've discussed so far, these types of books benefit from the three main concepts and the resulting touchpoints. However, there are a few extra tips that are particularly important for those who are writing philosophy or analysis books.

Specifically, I'd like to devote a couple of chapters to what it means to write a book that comes entirely from your own head... yet is 100% factual.

Uploading Brain-Share Material

Philosophical and insight books are unique—while you still need to have well-researched facts as the basis for your discussion, the rest of the material is based on your own insight and expertise.

This does not mean you get to skip the research step. In fact, you'll likely want to make sure you're well-informed about your topic before you get started. While you may feel confident waxing on about your favorite analysis of a certain situation, you should also actively avoid creating a stream-of-consciousness disaster. Your best tools here are focus, clarity, and knowing the point you're trying to prove.

Each of these tools links directly back to our three concepts of topic, perspective, and organization.

Reflect back on our discussion about rabbit holes and details. While we addressed those topics in the context of history and travel books, I hope you can also see how running off on every possible tangent might unintentionally confuse the reader of a philosophical or analytical text.

"Focus" means keeping the readers' attention on one idea at a time, and giving them the details necessary to process each step and climb each ramp in a way that makes sense. Focus is a direct descendant of organization and perspective. If your notes and outline are organized in such a way that each of your talking points flows into the next, then you won't have to jar your readers with nonsequiturs, asides, and detours to help them understand what you're talking about.

"Clarity" is a sense of maintaining the same style, level of detail, measurement in steps, and language throughout your text to ensure the reader is able to follow your train of thought. That means putting aside what you understand and how you understand it and making sure that you're communicating your knowledge in a way that others can follow.

When I work on books, I generally go into a state of semi-seclusion so I can focus on the topic and the perspective I've chosen. If I start talking to too many people, I start incorporating their voices and views into my writing, so it's best to stay on the path until I'm done. After a while, I started getting a little desperate to talk to other people, so I asked my friends and family if they'd like to read an excerpt of my book. I do this for two reasons—first because I want to be able to talk about my book with someone in order to feel my way through some of the sticky parts, but also because I want to make sure I haven't created a messy stream-of-consciousness rant. There comes a point where writing a book can kind of feel like talking to yourself through a computer screen, especially if your goal is to share your point of view with others.

Whether you choose to share snippets of your book with others or enlist the help of a paid beta reader or editor, it's helpful to have another pair of eyes scan through the text to help you uncover whether your focus has been as tight as you've expected, and where the clarity stumbles off the path into the obscure.

Then comes "knowing the point you're trying to prove." This may seem a little obvious at first, but if you've ever heard an extremely drunk person try to communicate a simple recollection, you can appreciate how sometimes we think we're staying on topic, but alas, our passion and excitement have caused us to take a leave of logic, and we are far, far off-topic.

When I was in eighth grade, my English teacher spent a significant amount of time teaching us how to write thesis papers. In these papers, we came up with a single statement that we wished to prove throughout our writing, and then each following section provided a fact that we argued as proof of our thesis statement.

Each day we wrote some sort of thesis statement. The minimum length was generally five paragraphs, but the topics covered grammatical rules, the books we were reading, a random poem that had been printed on the chalkboard, or even a short film watched at the start of class.

Writing a philosophy, insight, or analytical book is not unlike constructing a very long thesis paper. While an exploration of certain tangents or rabbit holes may be warranted as part of the journey, you want to be sure that each paragraph supports your thesis statement. Everything you write should be placed on the page with the intention of proving that your point is valid and that delving into this topic with a trusted authority like yourself is a worthy investment of your readers' time.

So, if you take a little extra time in the topic development stage, or revisit your organization stage every time you sit down to write, rest assured that this is time well spent in order to help your audience explore your understanding of this topic with you.

Making People Care

I debated over the title of this chapter for a while because I feel it comes across as too blunt. I couldn't think of another way to say it though. When you're writing a philosophical or insight piece, you need to consider how you're going to find and fascinate your audience.

The reader and the writer have an unusual relationship. The writer has control of the book—the entire experience is in their hands when it comes to what's in the book. The reader has absolutely no say in the matter, and they are at the mercy of the writer when receiving the content for which they have paid.

However, writers, this does not mean you have an unwavering captive audience! Have you ever been to a party or event, and someone starts speaking to you... but never stops? They blather on relentlessly, showing no sign of fatigue as you grow increasingly restless.

When we fear we're being held hostage in person, we often find a polite—if not weak—reason to excuse ourselves from the situation before we reach our breaking point. When readers feel even slightly confused or bored, they close the book, set it down somewhere, and forget about it until they find it again during a thorough house cleaning.

Depending on your literary ambitions, this scenario may not trouble you, and that's fine. What I'm trying to establish is that you have just a small window in which to keep your readers' attention. There are countless books to read and infinite other things a person could spend their time doing—why should they spend precious time reading your book if it's not benefiting them in some way?

Folks can debate endlessly about how much an author "owes" a reader in terms of creating an ideal reading experience. Some say that you lose your integrity as a writer if you pen your books with the intent of curating and maintaining a loyal following. Others believe being authentic to your vision is meaningless if no one is reading your work.

I encourage everyone to develop their own appreciation and understanding of the roles of the reader and writer, especially as you explore both roles yourself. My personal goal is to find a sweet spot where you, the reader, will be both entertained and inspired by my books, even if you don't necessarily learn anything new. I'm here to promote confidence and try new things, not write a best-seller or start a cult. That being said, if you have read and enjoyed my entire catalog, I appreciate you, and thank you for joining me on this journey!

"Making people care" isn't a sworn duty, personal responsibility, or even a technical aspect that can be taught in writing classes. It manifests through an interesting perspective, maintains through impeccable organization, maneuvers the reader along a winding path with detail and format, and mesmerizes them with tone and clarity.

In my opinion, the best way to learn how to write a nonfiction book is to try it yourself. You can start small by doing exercises over and over again. You can write a little bit each day. Or, you can do what I did and accidentally fall into a job of rewriting a 30,000-word piece you were editing as your first major book-writing job and frantically flail about for the next 20 days, pulling in every possible resource to prevent you from failing. I don't recommend it, but it does help with perhaps increasing the amount of time you chain yourself to the desk (metaphorically, of course) as your capacity and curiosity or motivational issues you might have!

I've been doing this for over 20 years, and I'm thrilled to say that even at this stage of the game, writing nonfiction pieces of any length gets "easier" each time. Though I'm not entirely sure that "easier" is exactly the right word. There are still moments when I curse my own literacy and wonder why I think I ought to get paid for doing this since I clearly have no idea what I'm doing. Generally speaking, a few (hundred) deep breaths later, I can scroll back to where I last remember things making sense, and use my understanding of all of the concepts, elements, and ideas of nonfiction to help me find my way back on path. I've tried different things, practiced various notions, and researched not only what I'm doing by how I'm doing it. As a result, I find it less frustrating and heartbreaking when I have to edit and rewrite myself back to cohesiveness.

At first, trying to do all of the things you've just read about at once will seem impossible. But as you practice, as you write, and most importantly, as you read your own work, you'll start to understand your own patterns. Even better—you'll learn to embrace them, enhance them, and make them your own unmistakable style.

CONCLUSION

"No, I don't want to read your book about how to write nonfiction. I could never write nonfiction. I'd just look at the page and write a sentence and be like, 'Yeah, I'm done.'"

The same friend from the Introduction and I were talking about this very book as I was finishing my first draft.

"What do you mean?" I asked coyly. "Nonfiction means it happened. You just have to write down what was done and said, right?"

He stared at me with the look of someone who had suddenly put two and two together to reach an amazing conclusion. Was nonfiction hard, or was it easy? What if it was somewhere in the mystical undefined world between "simple" and "difficult?"

I looked at him, bemused. "Chocolate?" I asked as I offered him a chunk of my candy bar. Silently, he shoved it in his mouth. "Better thee than me," he replied with a sigh.

I like to help people out. I like to share information, but I like to do so in a way that's meaningful for the person on the receiving end of that information. I have absolutely been that person who holds one-sided conversations at parties (usually unintentionally), and I recognize that I have a lot of passion that needs to be carefully directed in order to be useful to anyone.

Having this mindset and personality is ideal for writing nonfiction books, though certainly, it is not a prerequisite. I would personally state that the only "requirement" for writing a nonfiction book is the desire to write a nonfiction book. Obviously, my friend has no desire to do so, so I wouldn't encourage him to try it. Life is too short to make yourself miserable!

However, if you have gotten through this book, and you're still interested in trying your hand at writing a nonfiction book of your own, please do. Start right now, tomorrow, or next week—whatever timeframe is logical for you. Think about your book. Think about where you want to take your readers (real or imagined), and what you want to cover. How will you bring glory to your topic? What revelations will you make? How many lives will change thanks to you placing your fingers on keys or paper and recording your own words?

That might seem to be an overly romanticized look at nonfiction, but really, it's quite true. Biographies, autobiographies, memoirs, historical pieces, travel books, self-help, how-to, philosophical, and analytical books have the power to inform, entertain, inspire, and encourage people to think or live differently than they do today. We read because we want to understand more perspectives and have adventures beyond our own. Almost everything we read has some sort of impact on us, whether by imparting knowledge, engaging our emotions, or moving us to make changes.

If you flip back to Chapter 1, you'll see some examples of the first notes and outlines I made for this book. You can compare this to the actual final table of contents, as well as your overall draft to demonstrate how things change and evolve in the process of writing a book.

I could have instructed you to follow a step–by–step process because it works perfectly for me, but that's not the how-to book I wanted to write. This is primarily because I don't follow a step-by-step process, and nothing works perfectly for me, ever. That being said, I don't feel qualified to tell everyone how to do something exactly. Instead, I want to guide you through how to start thinking about it. How to engage your brain to consider the important ideas involved, rather than forcing you through processes that might not work for your way of learning, understanding, and doing.

We have covered so much material, and we've looked at many different concepts from different angles. It may be hard to put all of these concepts together until you have the chance to try them out yourself. I've always said that writing is like staring at the world with kaleidoscope attachments on a pair of binoculars, and after reading this, you might understand that metaphor a little more!

I hope that you are inspired to work on your own nonfiction book. I hope you complete the exercises and continue to practice. Whether you are boldly passionate about your work or begrudgingly accepting that writing is something that ultimately gives you great joy despite its many frustrations, I hope you always strive to learn and grow in your own writing.

Now write on!

RESOURCES

As with my other books, I've included a handful of resources. Per reader request, I've categorized them by their relevancy to each section. So, all of the resources for Chapter 2 are grouped together, Chapter 3 together, etc. Fear not—I've labeled them so you aren't blindly clicking on links looking for something vaguely helpful!

Once again, I need to mention that I have no affiliation with any of these resources—I've chosen them strictly based on the fact that I feel they might be helpful for those who are interested in more information on the various concepts I've mentioned in this book.

I also encourage you to use these resources as the entrance to your own research rabbit hole. As writers, we are constantly learning and growing, and sometimes hearing the perspectives of those who have walked in similar shoes, so to speak, can be endlessly helpful—or at least sympathetic!

Enjoy!

General Resources

These are resources that can be helpful for anyone who is brand new to the nonfiction scene.

"How to Write a Book (with Tactics from Best Sellers)"

https://blog.reedsy.com/how-to-write-a-book/

"How to Write a Nonfiction Book: A Step-by-Step Guide for Authors"

https://www.ingramspark.com/blog/how-to-write-a-nonfiction-book-guide-for-author
s

"The New Outliers: How Creative Nonfiction Became a Legitimate, Serious Genre"

https://lithub.com/the-new-outliers-how-creative-nonfiction-became-a-legitimate-
serious-genre/

SEO Tools - For those who are interested in doing keyword analysis or demographic searches, these pages dive into various tool options and how they work.

Ahrefs: https://ahrefs.com/blog/free-seo-tools/

Semrush: https://www.semrush.com/blog/free-seo-tools/

Forbes Advisor: https://www.forbes.com/advisor/business/software/best-seo-software

Chapter 2

For this section, I wanted to share a few different perspectives from writers and publishing companies on what it takes to write biographies, autobiographies, and memoirs. I encourage everyone to check out writing blogs such as these not as a way to compare yourself to others, but to gain a feel for how all writers deal with challenges differently, and take inspiration and hope from what they share.

"Autobiography vs. Biography vs. Memoir"

https://www.blurb.com/blog/memoirs-biographies-autobiographies/

"How To Write An Autobiography, A Biography and Memoir."

https://www.creativewritingnews.com/how-to-write-an-autobiography-a-biography-an
d-memoir/

"How to Write a Biography: 8 Steps for a Captivating Story"

https://www.tckpublishing.com/how-to-write-a-biography/

"How to write an autobiography: 7 key steps"

https://www.nownovel.com/blog/how-to-write-autobiography/

"Memoir vs. Autobiography: Which Should You Write?"

https://www.dudleycourtpress.com/memoir-vs-autobiography-which-should-you-write/

Chapter 3

These resources specifically help writers connect history and nonfiction, as well as put their travels into words.

"Six Ways a Historian Can Help You Write a Nonfiction Book"

https://www.thewritersforhire.com/six-ways-a-historian-can-help-you-write-a-nonfiction-book/

"Writing Historical Fiction Vs. Creative Nonfiction | Writer's Relief"

https://writersrelief.com/writing-historical-fiction-vs-creative-nonfiction-writers-relief/

"8 Travel-Writing Tips From Professional Travel Writers"

https://www.grammarly.com/blog/travel-writing-advice/

"Cathedral," by Raymond Carver (as mentioned as an example)

http://www.giuliotortello.it/ebook/cathedral.pdf

Chapter 4

Here you'll find a few interesting selections for those interested in writing self-help and how-to books. You may find that the ideas in these links can apply to each type of book!

"A Guide to Writing Self-Help"

https://nybookeditors.com/2017/06/guide-writing-self-help/

"The 3 Golden Rules Of Writing A Self-help Book"

https://www.standoutbooks.com/how-to-write-a-self-help-book/

"How to Write a "How To" Book By Susan Bilheimer"

https://writersweekly.com/this-weeks-article/how-to-write-a-how-to-book-by-susan-bilheimer

Chapter 5

And lastly, look at philosophical and insight/analysis pieces. You'll find these links come from academic resources. Given that philosophical and insight pieces have a background in educational environments, it stands to reason that some of the strongest guiding hands in these areas are actual educators. Don't let words like "paper" or "literary" throw you off—I felt the concepts in these resources were strong enough to benefit book writers such as yourself!

"A Brief Guide to Writing the Philosophy Paper"

https://philosophy.fas.harvard.edu/files/phildept/files/brief_guide_to_writing_philoso phy_paper.pdf

"A Short Guide to Close Reading for Literary Analysis"

https://writing.wisc.edu/handbook/assignments/closereading/

REVIEWS

Reviews and feedback help improve this book and the author. If you enjoy this book, we would greatly appreciate it if you could take a few moments to share your opinion and post a review on Amazon. Thank you!

ALSO BY LAUREN BINGHAM

One Word at a Time: How to Write a Fiction Book for Beginners

Just Write: A Calming, Realistic, and Optimistic Approach to Writing Your First Book

DOWNLOAD YOUR FREE 5 WRITING EXERCISES NOW!

If you're interested in learning to write books, chances are high that you've tried before and gotten stuck. As a result, you may be even less enthusiastic about trying again. If that's the case, check out some personally selected writing exercises from author Lauren Bingham's vault of helpful tricks and tips for getting the cursor moving again... or for the first time. Go to https://subscribepage.io/5-Writing-Exercises to download your own copy of Lauren Bingham's Five Favorite Writing Exercises.